Vannessa Uhlein
Neele Claussen

The Art of Gaining and Retaining Customers

Effective Implementation of Marketing Tools

VDM Verlag Dr. Müller

Bibliographic information by the German National Library: The German National Library lists this publication at the German National Bibliography; detailed bibliographic information is available on the Internet at http://dnb.d-nb.de.

Contact: info@vdm-verlag.de
Cover image: www.purestockx.com
Publisher: VDM Verlag Dr. Müller e. K., Dudweiler Landstr. 125 a, 66123 Saarbrücken, Germany
Produced by: Lightning Source Inc., La Vergne, Tennessee/USA
        Lightning Source UK Ltd., Milton Keynes, UK

Bibliografische Information der Deutschen Nationalbibliothek: Die Deutsche Nationalbibliothek verzeichnet diese Publikation in der Deutschen Nationalbibliografie; detaillierte bibliografische Daten sind im Internet über http://dnb.d-nb.de abrufbar.

Kontakt: info@vdm-verlag.de
Coverbild: www.purestockx.com
Verlag: VDM Verlag Dr. Müller e. K., Dudweiler Landstr. 125 a, 66123 Saarbrücken, Deutschland
Herstellung: Lightning Source Inc., La Vergne, Tennessee/USA
        Lightning Source UK Ltd., Milton Keynes, UK

ISBN: 978-3-8364-1053-3

Table of Contents

Table of Figures

1 Introduction

"Sales Promotions are unique in their ability to respond in quick, focused and flexible ways to motivate consumers [...]. These flexible-rapid response, market targeting characteristics of sales promotions are particularly well suited promotional tools for this technological age of worldwide communication, rapid innovations in technology and intense competition." [1]

1.1 Background

Since the beginning of the industrialization, the worldwide economy has been steadily growing. During this process, single national markets have converted into intertwined multinational exchanges with arising difficulties for companies in finding and maintaining their place in the global economy. This development on the one hand opened up several opportunities concerning new potential customers and cheaper production or supply facilities, but on the other hand enforced fierce competition between providers of goods and services.

Noticeably, the consumer behaviour in developed countries has also changed in this economic process. First of all, because the majority of his material needs, such as having a full-equipped household, cars and clothes have been satisfied; and secondly, the customer now has the possibility to choose from a wide range of products offered by various providers to satisfy the daily needs for perishables as well as occasional needs for renewals, replacements and product innovations.

As a result of this increasing market saturation it is getting harder for companies to meet their sales objectives and with that ensure the survival of the enterprise. On top of that, it is becoming more and more complicated to attract the today's customers' attention, as they are daily exposed to a huge quantity of impulses. People "are bombarded with many hundreds of advertisements every day"[2], this means it is nearly impossible to perceive all given information and they therefore only filter out the important one and ignore the rest.

At this point emerges the challenge for Marketing, namely to arise the stimulus satiated customer's interest in the product. The traditional tool of advertising has lost parts of its effectiveness over the years as consumers have learned to be more attentive. "They have unprecedented access to information and are less likely to swallow what they hear from marketers."[3] Hence, the growing tendency towards two alternative methods, **Sales Promotion and Relationship Marketing**, is to be found. Companies are shifting shares within the promotion budget from mass media advertising to promotional in-and-out-store campaigns and lay stronger emphasis on binding the customer on the long run.[4]

---

[1] Srinivasan, S., Anderson, R.; Concepts and strategy guidelines for designing value enhancing sales promotions
[2] Statt, David A., Understanding the Consumer, p. 47
[3] http://www.marketingtoday.com/marketing/0905/relevant_marketing.htm
[4] Kotler, P., Marketing Management, p.597 ff.

1.2 Problem formulation

To find out if this current tendency is recommendable, we asked ourselves how consumers react to these methods, especially towards sales promotion. Are they really interested in the product when they receive a sample or do they rather like the idea of obtaining something for free? How do brand-loyal customers react on promotions?

Knowing peoples' attitudes can help companies to divide their advertising budget more efficiently and to save money. We therefore would like to detect

1) **If Sales Promotion really is an effective instrument to influence the customer in his decision-making process.**

2) **If the creation of a long-lasting relationship between a company and a customer is appreciated or seen as rather annoying by the clients.**

3) **Whether it is possible to connect the short-term Sales Promotion instruments with the long-term Relationship Marketing approach effectively.**

1.3 Aim of the study

With our thesis we would mainly like to investigate today's effectiveness of sales promotion tools in Germany by exploring consumers' attitudes towards them. We would like to call attention to the effective implementation of promotion tools and relationship marketing concerning their impact on the customer's decision-making process. Furthermore, we aim to search for possible connection strategies linking short-and-long-term marketing methods and analyse their popularity.

1.4 Limitations

In the course of our work we will only treat promotion methods targeted at end-consumers in order to avoid an overload of information, which would have been caused by considering sales promotion aimed at retailers as well. Furthermore, we will concentrate on a selection of tools, which seemed most suitable in respect to our research purpose.

1.5 Disposition

After introducing our research topic, including the research problem and its delimitations in Chapter 1, the second Chapter delivers the theoretical basis for our study.

Chapter 2 is divided into five parts. It starts with a general overview and definition of sales promotion, describes its purpose and objectives and shows a selection of different promotion methods related to our research questions, as well as their advantages and disadvantages. Further, the concept of relationship marketing is introduced and compared to transactional marketing. In addition, its benefits and situations of inadequacy are stated. The third part treats the customer's purchase-decision-making process and how can it be influenced by marketing. The term deal-proneness is explained in order to understand customers' affinity towards certain promotion tools. Former studies on this topic are presented in the forth section and lastly the research model will be presented which will be developed on the basis of the shortcomings of former research.

In the 3rd Chapter we will describe our research design including the approach, the strategy and our data collection method. Further, the reliability and validity of our study are discussed. Chapter 4 will provide the reader with our empirical findings, which will then be analysed and compared to the theory. Finally, in Chapter 5 we will discuss the results and present our conclusion.

2 Marketing Concepts and the Customer

A business can only be maintained by making profits. The company's survival depends to a great extent on the sales figures, and expensive but inefficient marketing activities can be mortal for an enterprise.

The traditional marketing concept embraces four main tools, namely the **4 P's**:

- product including features as packaging and design
- price,
- place (distribution channels) and
- promotion activities as advertising or sales promotion.[5]

This kind of marketing is rather focused on **transactions** than on lasting relations with the customers. Therefore new concepts are developed to retain consumers on the long run. But still the first obstacle that has to be overcome is to convince the consumer to purchase our product.

In the following, **sales promotion** –a traditional tool which aims at attracting new customers – and **relationship marketing** as a new approach to maintain the existing clientele will be introduced. Furthermore, we will present an overview of consumer's behaviour and attitudes – the **purchase decision-making process** and **deal proneness** – with the purpose of revealing the influence of these two marketing methods on the customer.

2.1 Sales Promotion

The notion sales promotion belongs together with advertising to the generic term of promotion, which "keeps the product in the minds of the customer and helps stimulate demand for the product. Promotion involves ongoing advertising and publicity (mention in the press). The ongoing activities of advertising, sales and public relations are often considered aspects of promotions."[6] Advertising then again is defined as "bringing a product (or service) to the attention of potential and current customers. Advertising is typically done with signs, brochures, commercials, direct mailings or e-mail messages, etc."[7] In order to distinguish sales promotion from advertising, it should be said that while advertising "appeals to the mind and emotions to give the consumer a *reason* to buy, sales promotion [...] provides an *incentive* for purchasing a brand"[8], namely an **added value**, which is mostly of material or financial nature.

In general, we can classify sales promotion into three types depending on the initiator and the target of the promotion.[9] The first one, Trade Promotion, refers to manufacturers' activities towards retailers, whereas Retailer Promotion and Consumer Promotion embrace actions directed to the end-consumer deriving from both, the retailer and the manufacturer. As above-mentioned, we will concentrate on the latter ones.

---

[5] Berná Pastor, N., Comportamiento del Consumidor
[6] http://www.managementhelp.org/ad_prmot/defntion.htm
[7] ibid
[8] Belch, George & Michael, Introduction to Advertising & Promotion, p 476
[9] Persson, P.-G., Modeling the impact of Sales Promotion on store profits, p 2

To give a concise definition, "sales promotion consists of a diverse collection of **incentive tools**, mostly **short-term**, designed to stimulate **quicker or greater purchase** of particular products or services by consumers"[10] and should not be seen as "a separate aspect of the promotion category of tools, but rather an underpinning bridge"[11] combining promotion with the variables product, price and place. It may change the packaging or reduce the price of a product and have effects on the participants of the distribution channel.

Companies more than ever focus on sales promotion activities to maximize their sales volume yet that advertising helps to transmit the brand image but not necessarily makes the audience buy the product immediately. Belch et al. speak of a decline in advertising expenditures from 43% of the marketing budget in 1981 to 25% in 1993.[12] Kotler supports this data, saying that nowadays sales promotion accounts for up to 75% of the marketing budget.[13]

2.1.1 Purpose and Objectives

Companies have to implement their promotion activities effectively to meet their sales objectives. Effectiveness "means the capability of, or success in, achieving a given goal"[14]. The main objectives manufacturers and retailers are striving to achieve are:

- *attract new customers*
- *increase brand awareness and*
- *increase sales to present customers.*[15]

Kotler replaces the objective increasing brand awareness by *rewarding loyal customers for their steady consume.*[16] A different source tells us that in researches effectuated during the early 1990s eight out of ten people were already loyal customers to a product and would have bought the product anyway.[17] Furthermore, Kotler states that within the group of new triers, promotion activities often attract brand switchers who are primarily looking for a favourable offer and probably will not turn into loyal users, as they do not care about brands in general. True customers of brands or product categories seldom react on competitor's promotion as they either do not perceive it or they are not interested in a change.

While trying to meet the aims, one has to be aware that sales promotions, if used too often, bear the risk of weakening brand loyalty as clients for example could get used to the lower price of the product and as a consequence only buy it when it is promoted. However, before deciding on the frequency one has to choose the matching tool for his purposes.

2.1.2 Tool box

In the following we will exemplify those sales promotion tools that seemed to us as the most relevant in view of the short-term vs. long-term contacts with consumers. First we chose **samples** and **coupons**, as they are classical and wide-spread promotion tools; second

---

[10] Blattberg and Neslin (1990), found in Persson, P.-G., Modeling the impact of Sales Promotion on store profits
[11] Varey, R., Marketing Communication
[12] ibid, p. 478
[13] Kotler, P., Marketing Management, p.597 ff.
[14] http://en.wikipedia.org/wiki/Effectiveness
[15] Blattberg and Neslin (1990), found in Persson, P.-G., Modeling the impact of Sales Promotion on store profits
[16] Kotler, P., Marketing Management
[17] Varey, R., Marketing Communication

premiums and **loyalty cards**, combining short-term incentives like little gifts with long-term relationship strategies as e.g. loyalty points; and third **sweepstakes** as a special way of promoting a brand as the aim is not to increase sales figures on the short but on the long run.

Samples are offers of a free amount of a product or service to make prospective customers try it[18]. They are often attached to other articles, distributed in stores, e.g. food products and those articles that need explanation, or handed out directly to a special target group like students, who often receive a bag full of samples at the semester start.

In general, sampling is the best method to make people try new products or brands as it is for free and without obligation[19]. It is a useful instrument because not all consumers are open for innovations, partly due to doubts concerning quality or taste, partly dominate the shopping habits. Prospective customers can experience the brand directly – often in a private atmosphere – which may make them feel more comfortable. Imagine you are given a sports car 24 hours to try it. What will your friends say? Can you renounce the car that easily? Lest companies waste unnecessary budget for customers trying but not buying the product, an efficient distribution is essential. Furthermore, companies have to think about an adjunct to stimulate repurchase to bind the customer.

Coupons are certificates entitling the bearer to a stated saving on the purchase of a specific product and can be spread by mail, attached to other products or can be obtained by the customer e.g. at the point of sale or personal promoters[20]. Besides the samples, this tool is used to generate early trial as it reduces the perceived risk of trying something unknown. Many new products include coupons inside the package to provide an incentive for repurchase.

The biggest advantage of coupons is the possibility to offer a price reduction without reducing it for everyone, but only to those customers who are price sensitive[21]. A further one is that it represents a chance for two types of brands: expensive ones might be affordable by everyone and mature or forgotten brands can stimulate repurchase. Within the disadvantages we can figure out that it often reduces profit margins as it mainly attracts loyal customers and does not provoke new trial to that degree than samples do. Since the response to a coupon is rarely immediate, it is difficult to estimate the extent and herewith the costs of use in advance. Another fact that can make us doubt the efficiency of coupons is the abuse, as employees could easily exchange them for cash and/or redeem them without buying the product.

Premiums are merchandise offered free or at a relatively low cost as an incentive to purchase a particular product[22]. Beside others, we find *with-pack premium,* like little gifts, inside the package or a *free-in-the-mail premium* on sending in a proof of one's purchase, for example fidelity points. A big advantage of this tool is the high impulse value, as people like to receive presents, which can positively influence the attitude towards a company[23].

Premiums are defined as consumer's favourite type of promotion and often encourage repeat purchase, which finally can lead to brand loyalty[24]. Another benefit for the enterprise is that they get to know the clients address in case of sending in loyalty points, which can be used for

---

[18] Kotler, P., Marketing Management
[19] Belch, George & Michael, Introduction to Advertising & Promotion
[20] Kotler, P., Marketing Management
[21] Belch, George & Michael, Introduction to Advertising & Promotion
[22] Kotler, P., Marketing Management
[23] ibid
[24] Belch, George & Michael, Introduction to Advertising & Promotion

promotion purposes afterwards. A big difficulty is finding desirable gifts for adults at reasonable prices that add value to the brand. Poor premiums can even harm it. In addition, there are probably a lot of customers lacking the effort to collect and mail back the bonus points.

Loyalty or Club Cards are plastic cards identifying the customer in certain retail stores as prerequisite to grant a discount right away or to collect points that can be used for future purchase[25]. It can be seen as a mixture of discounts, coupons and premiums.

Emitting these cards is a current trend due to its obvious advantages: The customer provides the company voluntarily with his address and with his shopping habits. This data can afterwards be used for internal statistics, as a basis for relationship marketing or for direct promotion purposes. For the customer it is more convenient not to have to cut out coupons or collect receipts as proof for a special offer.[26] A critique is that people feel observed because they are the target of a lot of direct mail advertising as a result of the marketing effort on the revealed information and they lose their interest in these cards[27]. One can also observe an increasing overload of these cards, which can confuse the customer.

Contests/Sweepstakes: A contest requires consumer's abilities and skills as their entry submitted will be examined and judged, whereas sweepstakes only call for participation via postcard or email. These kinds of promotion have a special appeal and glamour and can even provoke excitement as it attracts people with amazing prizes or funny games[28]. In both cases purchase is not a prerequisite for participation, hence they cannot be used as a quick sales-fix but only to improve the image of the company.

Sweepstakes are more favourable than contests as they are easier to enter for the customer and cheaper for the manufacturer, as they do not have to evaluate every entry[29]. Nevertheless, in a contest the involvement is usually higher and therefore the possibility to create brand awareness. In both cases the supplier is provided with the customer's address and maybe more personal information like special interests, which can be used for marketing purposes afterwards. However, there is still the danger that people are only interested in the prize and not in the emitting company, as there are a lot of hobby sweepstakers. Furthermore, we have to cope with abuse e.g. by hackers who might crack the winning code.

Having presented the five chosen sales promotion tools – which are rather short-term orientated – the relationship marketing approach will be defined as follows, which puts emphasis on creating a bond between customer and company on the long run.

---

[25] http://en.wikipedia.org/wiki/Loyalty_card
[26] http://www.democratandchronicle.com/apps/pbcs.dll/article?AID=/business
[27] ibid
[28] Kotler, P., Marketing Management
[29] Belch, George & Michael, Introduction to Advertising & Promotion

2.2 Relationship Marketing

"Relationship marketing is the on-going process of **identifying and creating new value with individual customers** and then sharing the benefits of this over a lifetime of association."[30]

This marketing concept depends on communication, as the aim is to bind the customer on the long run by satisfying completely his demands. In today's business world it is important to retain existing customers because they can choose from a wide offer of providers and establishments and a lost client might never come back. An essential aspect of the relationship approach is the recruitment and training of employees in order to treat the customers according to their needs without harassing them to buy. As a motivated personnel is more likely to please clients, one model implemented in this context is empowerment, giving employees more responsibility e.g. a certain freedom in decision-making.[31]

2.2.1 Relationship vs. Transactional Marketing

While the transactional focus with its 4Ps basically consists of single sales operations and discontinuous customer contacts, relationship marketing adds a fifth dimension, namely people, and focuses on customer retention and stable customer contacts. It is not an entirely new concept but rather builds up on traditional marketing, strengthening the aspect of achieving and providing an "extra" for the clients through the effort of the whole company and not only the marketing division.

According to Grönroos, transactional marketing makes no, or only little, distinction between first-time and long-standing customers as everyone is treated as a prospect for canvassing, even if they have already traded and established a bond.[32] In contrary, the relationship approach is based on interaction. The aim is to **identify the individual customers, collect data concerning their habits, preferences, needs and interests and to act upon these answers**. Complaints are seen as opportunities to improve the systems and services, and with that the customer's satisfaction.

2.2.2 Benefits and Inadequacy

The benefits of relationship marketing are first of all lower costs of recruiting customers. While in the traditional approach the advertising budget is spend to attract consumers and to convince them to buy the product, the new strategy works with a selection of already satisfied clients and directs the investment more efficiently to promotion according to the identified needs.[33] Furthermore, it is known that pleased customers get more profitable as they are likely to purchase superior quantities in the course of time. Due to their satisfaction, they also become less price-sensitive and enable the supplier to raise his prices without losing the customer immediately. Content clients can as well function as a competitive advantage for a company since they are less driven to switch the supplier and could present an entry barrier to emerging competitors. Another advantage is that long-term customers are prone to initiate positive word-of-mouth and recommend the company to others, which can be seen as one of the most effective ways of advertising and should be aimed for by every enterprise.[34]

---

[30] http://www.converge.on.ca/itm00049.htm
[31] Payne, A. et al., Relationship Marketing for Competitive Advantage, Winning and Keeping Customers
[32] Grönroos (1990) found in Varey, R., Marketing Communication
[33] Varey, R. Marketing Communication
[34] Payne, Relationship Marketing for Competitive Advantage, Winning and Keeping Customers

However, there are also situations in which relationship marketing on the first sight seems not very suitable. For example for commodity product providers it is quite difficult to adopt a relationship marketing strategy because their customers have little reason to remain loyal to a single provider. They routinely search for the most accessible lowest-cost product supplier.[35] Nevertheless, more and more commodity product companies are trying to gain customer's loyalty by well-directed mailings or by special reward programs like loyalty-cards. As one can see, the relationship approach also has an influence on the promotional tools.

According to Kotler, whether a relationship approach is adequate or not depends on three dimensions: *the product, the provider and the customer. Products* that require a high customer involvement are more suitable while those, whose changes do neither imply risks or uncertainties, are less appropriate. The *provider* who is laying emphasis on differentiation and value-creation is obviously more adequate for implementing relationship marketing than the one whose competitive advantage is only based on costs. Concerning the *customer*, it is important to know whether he is valuing exchanges and relationships or if his orientation is only towards transactions and short-term business. In the next section, we are going to take a closer look at the consumer.

2.3 The Customer

The customer is the centre of all economic action; therefore a detailed analysis of his characteristics and preferences is the prerequisite for economic success and the survival of an enterprise. Hence, companies not only have to investigate the purchase actions, namely sales figures, but to include consumer's pre-and post purchase evaluation as part of the buying process.

2.3.1 Purchase decision-making process

A basic model of consumer decision-making is to be found in Belch et al (1995).

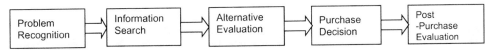

Figure 1: Purchase decision-making process

The decision-making process consists of five phases, which are always carried out but to a lesser or greater degree regarding to the importance or the value of the goods in question. In the course to come to a decision, the consumer is influenced by *internal and external factors.*[36] Whereas internal ones deal with individual and psychological issues, the latter ones are composed of the macro environment as e.g. technology on one hand and of the social environment as culture, social class or reference groups as friends or family members on the other hand. For sure, the marketing also exerts influence on the consumer.

Going closer into the process, the consumer first of all has to be **aware of his desires and needs**, which vary, among other things, according to one's personality and lifestyle.[37] Furthermore, he has to be motivated to change his current situation into the desired one, if not, no buying action will take place. Therefore, the marketing department has to think of

---

[35] Kotler (1991) found in Varey, R., Marketing Communication
[36] Belch, George & Michael, Introduction to Advertising & Promotion
[37] Berná Pastor, N., Comportamiento del Consumidor

target-specific advertising to arise attention and create awareness of a need among these individuals. In the first step, companies can make use of the synergy effects between advertising and sales promotion as an advertising campaign informs the consumer about the existence of a product and e.g. samples reduce the fear of trying something new.

Second, he will **search for information** about the product including features like brand and price.[38] If the already known data is not sufficient, he will make an effort to receive more details from external sources. The customer now perceives promotion instruments regarding the desired good more consciously – therefore flyers and coupons, which formerly might have been thrown away, will be studied carefully. The marketing department has to plan well where and how to distribute these instruments.

Once provided with all the facts needed, the consumer will **evaluate the alternatives** looking for the maximum benefit according to his desires.[39] Here, attitudes are formed upon former promotional tools, personal experience and word-of-mouth. The customer creates an *evoked set* of all the brands he is aware of and which are identified as purchase options.[40] At this point, relationship marketing can help to make one's product resistant against competitor's promotion attacks. Precisely this step is of interest for psychologists and marketers as heuristics loom large. Heuristics are mental shortcuts that help us to evaluate information faster and easier.[41] An example would be, that we associate expensive products with high quality. This connection between the price and the quality of a product is very delicate, as customers might also devalue the quality of an item, which is promoted too often.

Now, the consumer is prepared for step number four: **the decision**. Although he may know exactly what he is going to buy, additional considerations like where and when to buy and how much money to spend might be necessary.[42] One has to keep in mind that the consumer can still be persuaded by marketing tools at this stage of the process, mainly by in-store promotion, as a purchase decision is not yet an actual purchase. Loyalty cards and relationship marketing can influence in the choice of the establishment. Accordingly, companies should not forget about the importance of friendly, competent and collaborative personnel.

The buying process does not end with the purchase. After the act of buying, there is still an important step left: the **post purchase evaluation**. While consuming or using the product, one judges the meeting of expectations and the satisfaction of the purchase.[43] Attitudes are either confirmed or have to be reformed. Therefore, special emphasis has to be put on quality and reliability of products since poor samples or cheap gifts can lead to negative word-of-mouth, which can be destructive for an enterprise. In contrary, a satisfied customer is the best advertising and is disposed to influence positively the opinion of his fellow men and above all will probably repurchase the product.

The challenge for the marketing department is to influence the consumer as often and as intensive as possible in the single phases of the decision-making process in order to convince him to buy, and above all, re-buy a product. However, the promotion efforts can be high but still depend, at last instance, on the attitude of the consumer towards them.

---

[38] ibid
[39] Berná Pastor, N., Comportamiento del Consumidor
[40] Belch, George & Michael, Introduction to Advertising & Promotion
[41] Berná Pastor, N., Comportamiento del Consumidor
[42] Belch, George & Michael, Introduction to Advertising & Promotion
[43] Berná Pastor, N., Comportamiento del Consumidor

2.3.2 Deal proneness

Deal proneness can be defined as "a **consumer's general inclination to use promotional deals** such as buying on sale or using coupons."[44] Knowing about the degree of customers' deal proneness towards certain marketing tools is essential for companies in order to implement them more efficiently.

We can say that deal-prone consumers are those, who alter their buying behaviour to gain the benefits of the promotion's incentive.[45] The proneness is determined by *economic or functional values* like savings and quality on the one hand and by *hedonic benefits* like entertainment or self-expression on the other hand.[46] The degree of the advantage depends on the people's personality and environment. Some may enjoy shopping and look for innovations and variety; these consumers are a good target for samples or premiums. Others are loyal to brands and establishments and are likely to collect fidelity points or use loyalty cards. Some may have financial or storage constraints, who will react more intensively on out-store promotions and again others are quality conscious, so they will probably appreciate free trials.

Furthermore, we can distinguish between *active* and *passive proneness*.[47] As the term already reveals, active proneness is connected with the inclination of the consumer's action in cutting out coupons or search interesting promotion. Passive proneness though refers more to in-store promotion, which is a good opportunity regarding people with lack of time. People only have to decide at the shelf if they want to make use of the promotion or not.

2.4 Former research

Once defined the three main fields of our study – *sales promotion, relationship marketing* and the *customer* – we searched for articles treating these topics with a clear emphasis on sales promotion and its effects on the sales volume in order to get an overview about already existing studies. We selected seven articles which seemed most important to us. Five of them present a general picture on sales promotion, whereby two were targeted at the German market. A further article concerning brand loyalty in Germany was chosen to detect its effects on promotion. The 7th study treats the effects of consumer's psychographic values upon deal proneness. The shortcomings of former research helped us to motivate our own study and to develop our research model.

2.4.1 In general

Out of several research-articles that treat the efficiency of Sales Promotion, the majority deals with the financial revenues for companies deriving from single promotion activities. Here the effects were measured through sales data before, during and after promotion activities, primarily using the checkout scanners in supermarkets. The results turned out to be positive, at least on a short-term perspective. Bawa & Shoemaker's study concerning samples strongly supports the notion that "free samples can generate long-term sales increases for new brands"[48]. A second one from Lewis on loyalty cards found out that "loyalty programs with cumulative point systems work better at generating future sales and retaining customers than a series of independent promotions"[49]

---

[44] http://www.marketingpower.com/mg-dictionary-view959.php
[45] Martinez and Montaner, The effect of consumer's psychographic variables upon deal-proneness
[46] ibid
[47] ibid
[48] Bawa K. and Shoemaker R., The Effects of Free Sample Promotions on Incremental Brand Sales
[49] Lewis M., The Influence of Loyalty Programs and Short-term Promotions on Customer Retention

However, **these articles are lacking the customer's point of view**. Well obviously, the authors have measured consumer response but rather in terms of figures than on personality traits. In this respect, some additional and to us more important articles, which take psychological aspects of customer behaviour into account, could be identified. Their approaches and results are briefly going to be illustrated in the following.

The researches deal with consumer demographics and lifestyles regarding their affinity and response to in-and-out-store promotion. Martinez and Montaner examine the effects of economic benefits, hedonic benefits and the costs of promotion (e.g. brand-loyalty, time pressure and storage space constraints) upon deal proneness.[50] Laroche et al. also treat the above-mentioned variables but furthermore take the cognitive dimension and its effect on deal sensitivity, meaning influences of information search and evaluation, into account.[51]

The outcomes were predominantly expected. Price conscious consumers for example are deal prone to any kind of promotion while quality conscious ones only react positive to a few ones. Customers who enjoy frequent brand switching are particularly attracted by in-store promotions and people who are brand loyal respond to "their" brands promotions but not to competitive ones. Time pressure seems to have a positive effect on promotions as they often shorten the time to make a decision. Persons with storage problems rather react upon out-store promotion. Additionally, information search plays a significant role in connection with coupons. Surprisingly, none of the articles could affirm any relation between customers' financial situation and their attitudes towards promotion.

2.4.2 Sales Promotion in Germany

In addition to those international studies, we were able to find others, which describe current attitudes towards sales promotion and brand loyalty in Germany. For instance, one research from a marketing consulting agency located in Wiesbaden concerning point-of-sale marketing states that more than 75% of their interviewed customers react on in-store promotions.[52] While women are more prone to special offers, men prefer free-trials of a product offered by promoters. As information sources for shopping serve: people's own experience (90%), special offers (86%), brand-name (63%), word-of-mouth (43%) and coupons (10%).

A second article, written by the Institution of Market-orientated Leadership (IMU), investigated the effectiveness of several promotion tools.[53] The prevailing usage of sales promotion by customers is ranging from 58% for samples, over bonus-packs, sweepstakes and premiums to 17% for coupons. Furthermore, the authors of this article found out that coupons have a better impact on customer recruiting than on additional acquisitions of a product, while samples are helpful to attract new customers, as well as brand-switchers and also encourage further purchase. However and above all, people see free samples as a fun-factor of their shopping trip. A similar result was obtained for sweepstakes as they are seen as entertaining by more than half of the consumers, but only 12.1% would buy a new product as a consequence of participating.

In Germany, brand-image seems to be more important to men than to women when a buying-decision has to be made.[54] Common reasons for sticking with one brand are a good price-

---

[50] Martinez and Montaner, The effect of consumer's psychographic variables upon deal-proneness
[51] Laroche et al., A model of consumer response to two retail sales promotion techniques
[52] Wiesbadener Marketingberatung UGW: POS-Marketing Report 2004
[53] Institut für Marktorientierte Unternehmensführung (IMU): Effective Sales Promotion
[54] Dpm-team: Markentreue-Studie

performance ratio (67.8%), own experience with the brand (64.9%), good quality (59%) and special services (4.4%). It was also discovered that brand-loyalty rises with a higher net-income. This article was able to give us a first approach to examine the influence of the financial status on shopping behaviour.

2.5 The research model

After having presented the concepts of sales promotion, relationship marketing and the customer's buying habits, we presented some realized studies to create an outline for our own research, comparing it to the theory and investigations. In all former studies mentioned we were able to detect a common shortcoming: they **hardly question re-buy effects provoked by sales promotion methods**. They mainly ask people about the usage of several promotion tools and about character-traits which lead to utilization, but not if for example consumers are likely to turn into clients after having received a sample of a new product. In addition, the emphasis is rather laid on financial than on psychological traits. Finally, **none of the authors drew a connection between sales promotions and the purchase decision-making process or to relationship marketing**.

Thus, we decided to collect primary data and developed the following research model:

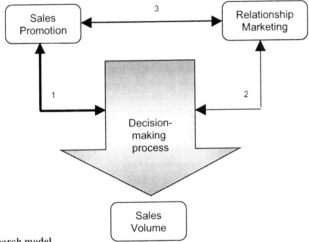

Figure 2: Research model

First, we were wondering whether it is possible to attract consumers and to enhance repurchase of an item with promotions that are offering primarily **material incentives** like samples, premiums or sweepstakes. We were curious to which degree customers are influenced by promotion in the early stages of the **decision process** e.g. by coupons, concerning where to buy and which brand to buy. As the emphasis of our research is laid on the effectiveness of sales promotion, the arrow is marked boldly. Second, we wanted to investigate the effects of **relationship marketing** on the final buying decision of end-consumers and third, its weight within promotion e.g. through loyalty-cards and direct mailings.

3 Method

Having established the base for the study in the introduction and the theoretical part, we will now give all necessary information on the chosen research method and the quality of our research.

3.1 Research design

The "research design is a master plan specifying the methods and procedures for collecting and analysing the needed information."[55] In the following we will explain the single steps of our research design that lead to the conduction of our study.

3.1.1 Approach

First of all, we decided to focus our primary data collection on only one market, namely the German one, as this is our home country. One criterion for specializing on this area was the fact that we know this market as well as marketing and promotion actions best. Another one was that we could reach our target population in our mother language, which made it possible to avoid misunderstandings due to language differences.

We then had to answer the question whether we want to opt for a qualitative or quantitative approach, as illustrated in figure 3. For the investigation of the effectiveness of sales promotion methods, it was imperative to collect a big amount of data, yet that it is a marketing tool directed to the mass and not to a single customer. We have therefore chosen a **quantitative method** in order to give a representative picture of customer behaviour through collecting as much information as possible. As we were also investigating attitudes, a **qualitative aspect** can be detected in the analytical, but not in the methodological part.

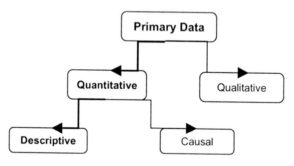

Figure 3: From primary data to the descriptive approach

Within the quantitative method, we had to decide whether we wanted to implement a descriptive approach for our study – which is used to describe characteristics of a population or a phenomenon when one is already aware of a problem but is lacking concrete evidence[56] – or a causal approach which in contrast identifies cause-and effect relationships among variables where the research problem has already been narrowly defined. As our basic research problem is the effectiveness of sales promotion in respect to consumer behaviour, we wanted to detect the characteristics and attitudes of our target population. We considered the

---

[55] Zikmund, W. G., Business Research Methods
[56] ibid

14

descriptive approach as the best suited technique for our purpose because we are conscious about the issue, but do not have sufficient information on customer's reactions towards certain promotion methods. The descriptive research will provide us with answers concerning who is prone to promotions, what methods are favoured, when and where promotion is most effective and how people behave in every-day shopping situations.

3.1.2 Strategy

After having decided for a descriptive approach, we needed to find the appropriate strategy for the collection of our primary data. An observation would have been rather difficult because on the one hand we are currently studying in Sweden and our target is located in Germany, and on the other hand it is not possible to observe the psychological reasons for buying or re-buying a product. Hence, we have selected the **survey** as the most suitable method. It made it possible to gain an inside on people's attitudes towards sales promotion and companies' tools to establish a relationship between these instruments and the customer, and at the same time provided us with the required demographical data of the respondents like profession and income.

As figure 4 shows, a survey can be conducted through interviews or a questionnaire. Due to the relatively short time frame, the questionnaire seemed more convenient to us. Here, we had the options to hand it out personally or to send it to the respondents via post or email. We made use of an **online self-administered questionnaire, which** allowed us to gather the necessary and relevant information in a quick and efficient way. In addition, it's a cost-saving method, which enabled us to reach a high number of participants without spending money for postal charges or telephone costs.

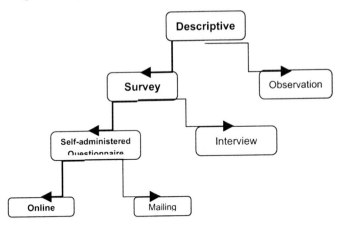

Figure 4: From the descriptive approach to an online-questionnaire

However, we are aware that the chosen method has a shortcoming. As the survey was conducted online, people without Internet access were excluded from it. According to a recent statistic, in Germany 63 % of all adults have access to the World Wide Web,[57] whereby the percentage reaches up to 80 for the age groups up to 50 years. Unfortunately, older population groups are difficult to reach because they hardly dispose of an Internet connection. Still, we saw it as a suited channel of distribution for our survey as we were sure that we could reach most people online.

---

[57] www.forschungsgruppe.de/Ergebnisse/ Internet-Strukturdaten/web_II_05.pdf

3.1.3 Questionnaire

In a **self-administered** questionnaire, the respondents can choose the moment in which they would like to fill it in. As they have enough time to consider their answers and are not influenced by an interviewer, we expect a high degree of people's honesty and accuracy in replying to the questions. A problem deriving from this method is that the respondent is responsible for reading and answering them and misunderstandings or interpretations can lead to invalid replies. This fact had a great impact on the question formulation. We therefore laid emphasis on a clear, understandable wording. Apart from one question, we avoided the use of open questions but focused on asking **closed questions** as well as giving precise answer possibilities. In order to avoid incomplete returns, we configured the questionnaire with **must-answers.**

The questionnaire (see appendix A) consists of three parts. The introductory part, questions 1-3, should detect the importance of several criteria in food and cosmetics as well as the necessity for samples before trying a product. We considered these questions as useful to get a general overview regarding customer's shopping preferences and further to compare them to the result of the attitudes in order to discover possible interdependencies between certain answers e.g. if people who often buy brands evaluate offers as important. The questions were formulated as matrix-questions and contain category scales, ranging in five steps from "very important" to "not at all important" as possible answers to guarantee the sensitivity of our measurement and with that a high comparability of the results.

The main part, questions 4-26, was designed to give information about customer's behaviour in respect to brand loyalty, relationship marketing and the five sales promotion methods mentioned before, namely samples, coupons, loyalty-cards, premiums and sweepstakes. This should help us to find out first, about reasons and frequencies of usage of the promotion tools and second, of their effectiveness by asking for potential changes in our respondent's attitudes after usage. The majority of these questions are category scales, giving three or five possible answers from one extreme behaviour e.g. "always" to another e.g. "never". Another type frequently used is multiple-choice questions where the respondents were asked to tick the most suitable statement. In question 25, we requested a ranking of the customer's favourite sales promotion method and finally, in question 26, an open question was posed to provide them with the possibility of giving their personal opinion on the topic.

Last but not least, questions 27-31 treat the demographic aspects gender, age, profession, income and children of our sample. This data will help us to link specific characteristics to certain groups of population and also will shed light on the representativeness of our studied population.

Before sending the questionnaire to our target group, it had to be **pre-tested**. The testing was made by German exchange-students and by our family members to cover a major part of the expected sample. Through this we were able to find out about possible comprehension problems due to question formulation. As a consequence, two questions were added and minor changes in editing were made.

As a last step the final version of the questionnaire was uploaded to a **website** and the link was sent to our sample via email. The persons were asked to respond as soon as possible and to forward the link to their family, friends and colleagues so as to make our study more representative yet that they reflect a wider range of age and occupation. Through the website we could avoid unnecessary down-and uploading processes of the questionnaire and so provide a more convenient way of responding. Another positive effect of this web page was our high response rate of 471 persons.

The results were collected and the basic statistics were directly evaluated on the website. Invalid responses due to incomplete questionnaires, partly because of server problems, had to be deleted. In one question (n°12) the programme failed and we had to calculate a new basis and the matching percentages. For further analysis we made use of **filters** and cross-tables available at the survey provider's homepage and the Microsoft programme Excel to illustrate and compare the obtained figures.

3.1.4 Sampling

One can distinguish between two types of sampling: *probability sampling*, in which every member of the population will have a known nonzero probability of selection, and *non-probability sampling*, where units of a sample are selected on the basis of personal judgement or convenience.[58] As the latter is rather subject to the researchers choice, it might not be appropriate to transfer the results to the whole population, but can still provide valuable information.

Due to the fact that we are currently geographically separated from our target population, our research sample started out as a **convenience sample**. We considered it the most effective way to email the link to the questionnaire to our friends, family, fellow students and former colleagues to reach many people, from which we could expect that they would respond to it within a short time frame. In total, the link was sent to about 130 persons, men and women in approximately equal shares, with the request to forward it as we also hoped to profit from a snowball effect.

When deciding on the sample, we knew that a convenience sample would not adequately represent all parts of the population. In our case, we expected it to over-emphasize the group of students, as they do not account for a major part of the German residents but for a big part of our contacts. As a logical consequence, the biggest age group would then consist of people between 20 and 30 years and the dispersion of the net-income might also distort towards the lowest income-class. Nevertheless, we do not see this as a big disadvantage because we consider young people as a good target group for our survey. To support this, we filtered the students and compared the results with the non-students. The differences tended to 0.

3.2 Research quality

The quality of a research is determined by the worth of its measurements. Whether measurements are useful or not depends mostly on their reliability and validity. In the following we will apply these two concepts on the results of our study.

3.2.1 Reliability

Reliability of a measurement instrument is given when the results of a research are reproducible.[59] This is the case, if the same, or a similar result can be attained at a different time or in a different testing-situation.

---

[58] Zikmund, W. G., Business Research Methods
[59] ibid

As we were basically investigating the attitudes and the behaviour of our sample towards certain sales promotion practices, it should be possible to obtain the same results in a second test within the same population. Customers' mindset will not change from one day to another, provided the fact that they do not gain extraordinary negative or positive experience meanwhile; we therefore consider our results as reliable.

One possible source for incomplete reliability could be the nature of our sample. Choosing a convenience sample limits the reproducibility for other investigators. They might not get the same results for their selected population.

3.2.2 Validity

Our questionnaire presumed to measure the effectiveness of determined sales promotion tools in Germany by detecting their influences on the purchase of a product or a change in attitudes due to promotion. **Construct validity** is given if the measurement shows the results that it is supposed to[60]. As the survey was conducted in German, we were able to use precise wording and through that obtain exact results. Only in one case we had a minor issue with a contradictory result for coupons, as we utilized two different expressions for it. The results in general though, do indeed give us information about customer's behaviour and attitudes towards sales promotion and reactions as a consequence of promotion methods. So, we can confirm high construct validity.

As far as the **internal validity** is concerned, it can be said that it is possible to establish causal relations among the questions. Especially, this can be done between the importance of certain criteria in the first two questions and consumer's attitudes towards the promotion tools later on, as for example brand-loyal customers do not consider offers as important as price conscious customers do.

In some questions, which built up on each other, the causal relation might be disturbed. Here, some respondents did not follow the instructions and answered a follow up question e.g. stating that the loyalty card influences them because they consider certain criteria as important or unimportant, although they responded that the card would never influence them in their store choice in the question anterior to this one. Therefore the internal validity is only partly assured.

We have already stated in the section about sampling that our study method is not completely free of biases. This fact weakens the **external validity,** as it might not be possible to generalize the results for other populations. The online survey might limit the validity because only people with an Internet connection/access could participate. Through that, especially older population groups and socially/economically weak persons might have been excluded. As we distributed the questionnaire mainly to students, we potentially have left out people with a lower educational background.

However, we could detect clear tendencies in the answers that represent a wide spectrum of age, professions and income-classes. Through that an external validity should, at least to a certain degree, be assumable.

---

[60] Zikmund, W. G., Business Research Methods

4 Analysis of the empirical findings

After explaining how our study has been conducted, this part of the paper will now present and analyse the results of our online-questionnaire. In total we received 471 responses from the German population and first of all we will illustrate this sample stating the **demographical data**. Second, the single promotion **tools** will be analysed, and third the results regarding the **decision-making process** will be interpreted. All results and percentages can be found in the **appendix B**, supplemented by the filters we worked with.

4.1 Demographics
(Questions 27-31, see appendix B)

The demographical categories questioned in the survey were gender, age, occupation, monthly net-income and the number of children living in a household. The division of **gender** took place in almost equal shares, whereby the survey ended up with a slight female domination of 58.2%. In the course of interrogation there were also days when we could count more male participation, so the final result is basically a product of chance.

Our respondents represent a wide range of **age**. The youngest person is 17 and the oldest one 61 years old. Nevertheless, as stated in the sampling part, the estimated majority of the participants consisted of the age group 20-30. Therefore, the median (the middle value in a series of numbers, which separates a row into two parts of the same size) is situated at 25 and the average age is 28,64 years.

Concerning the **occupation** (see figure 5), we gave six possibilities to choose from to generalize profession groups. As expected, the biggest subgroup with 45.0% is composed of students, followed by employees with 39.9%. The third largest population is represented by the self-employed with 5.3%. Trainees, unemployed people and other professions account for the remaining 9.8%.

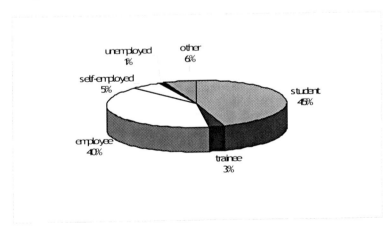

Figure 5: Occupation

As a consequence of the results for age and occupation, more than half of the participants dispose of a **monthly net-income** inferior to 1,000€ (figure 6). Almost one third of the respondents earn between 1,000€ and 2,000€ a month, and 10.8% receive a salary between 2,000€ and 3,000€. Only 8.1% possess more than 3,000€ a month.

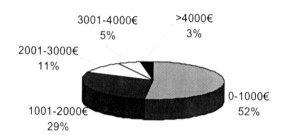

Figure 6: Net-income per month [in €]

The last demographic question was about the number of **children** within the household. We considered this fact as interesting because of possible variations in shopping attitudes of families with many children and childless households. Unfortunately, in 85.4% of the households interrogated do not live any children. This makes a valid comparison almost impossible because only 7.2% are one-child-households, 5.5% live with two children in their homes and only in 9 households interviewed are currently living three or more children. Hence we refrained from filtering the influence of children in buying behaviour.

4.2 Effectiveness of promotion tools

First, we will analyse the outcomes for each of the five promotion activities and second, we will give an overview of customer's preferences regarding the tools.

4.2.1 Samples
(Questions 3-8, see appendix B)

It is known that free samples are a frequently used tool to make people try new products and through this arise interest in them. Companies also implement samples in order to lower customer's fear factor regarding the unknown. We were curious how strong this fear factor really is and therefore asked our respondents how important they would consider testing a product before buying it. This question (n°3) had a matrix structure for 9 product categories (6 food and 3 non-food) and the answer possibilities "very important", "important", "neutral", "rather unimportant" and "not at all important".

The outcomes for **testing** a product – e.g. drinks, snacks and bakery – range from "very important" to "not at all important" with a focus on "neutral" or "rather unimportant" in the food categories. One can see that at least for edibles or cheaper, low involvement products the fear of buying bad quality or taste is not that high. In the three non-food groups, namely hygiene/cosmetic, software/internet-provider and newspaper/magazines, the majority (39.1-42.9%) considered it as important to test a product before buying it. The female answers dominated for the cosmetic products, while men prefer to test newspapers. The results for those groups show us that people seem to be more cautious when it comes to products where they put high expectations on the quality and which require a higher customer involvement. Furthermore, we wanted to detect people's **attitudes** towards free samples. From former research we know that 58% of the German customers use them and that it is seen as an effective tool to gain new customers. In concrete, we wanted to find out whether customers take samples because they are really interested in the product or just because they obtain something for free. Additionally, we were interested if customers purchase the product after having been convinced by a sample.

Question n°4 aimed at their **reason** for collecting them. Out of five answer possibilities ranging from "always" to "never" most of the respondents (42.5%) say that they often take them because they are interested in their taste or quality. The dominating answer for "I take them because they are for free" is also "often". Here it was noticeable that for the female population the main answer is "always" (33.9%). This result contradicts the statement of the POS-study saying that men react more on free trials than women. New products are also often (38.4%) a reason for picking up samples. Comparing the averages of the results we can see that the most frequent reason to take them is because they are for free. This reflects that samples are rather seen as a fun factor of the shopping trip, providing hedonic benefits. People like to try products, although in most cases they do not consider it as necessary or very important.

We were also asking whether people knew **websites** that offer free samples (n° 6-8) and in case of yes, if and why they use it. Given the fact that 72.2% do not know the pages and out of the remaining 27.8% who knew them almost 60% never used them, the results for the usage of those sites are not that significant. Within the third using these pages, reason number one for visiting them was "obtaining something for free" closely followed by "I like to surf on the Internet" and "interest in new products". The fourth graded reason was "due to convenience".

If a received sample convinced a customer, the probability of **purchasing the product** was parted within our respondents as illustrated in figure 7. 28.1% always or often acquire it, 17.6% seldom or never decide for a purchase. More than half of the respondents sometimes buy it. We can see that samples are effective to attract clients.

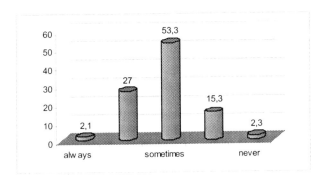

Figure 7: Question 5 – Purchase probability

21

4.2.2 Premiums
(Questions 19 & 20, see appendix B)

According to the theory, a big advantage of premiums is their high impact value as people like to receive gifts and it is stated as consumer's favourite type of promotion. In order to get an inside on people's interest in premiums we asked them in n° 19 if they would decide to buy a magazine/newspaper only because of an extra attached to it. Almost three quarters of the participants quote that they seldom or never do it. 5.7% admit to purchase it often and 20.2% sometimes because of the premium. For just 3 persons it is always the reason to choose a journal. Although magazines often carry attached premiums, it was probably not the best choice to measure the effectiveness of premiums, yet that people usually put more emphasis on magazine's contents than on the gift.

However, in question n° 20 we asked for the **motive to select a product** when there are two equivalent ones and received similar results for the premium. Only 8.7% saw it as an incentive for purchase. It is interesting though, that this small group, consisting to four fifth of women, seems to react stronger on promotion in general. For example more than 48% of them always or often buy a product after being convinced of a product due to a sample (see filter 20.1). In addition, the percentage of people saying that they are very interested in collecting and redeeming coupons is almost twice as high as the average vote (9.8% contrary to 5.5%). Moreover, 19.5% admit that the premium is often or always a reason to buy a magazine (average 6.3%).

In total, and in comparison to the other promotion tools, the premium in form of a gift does not seem to be a popular incentive. A possible reason for their unpopularity might be that there is a problem to find suitable items for adults.

4.2.3 Coupons
(Questions 13, 15, 25, see appendix B)

The IMV – Effective Sales Promotion research about the prevailing usage of sales promotion in Germany quotes that coupons are used by 17% of the population. Our findings about coupons turned out to be somehow contradictory in itself. In question n° 15 about people's interest in collecting and redeeming coupons we found out that nearly half of the respondents (45.2%) are not at all interested in them. Only 5.5% signalise a strong interest and the remaining half takes few stock in coupons.

Nevertheless, in question n° 25 asking for customer's favourite promotion tool, coupons/vouchers represent the best-liked tool and in connection to loyalty cards they are often considered as an important cause for the store choice (n° 13). One possible reason for this contradiction could be that for the ranking respondents did not consider the fact that they might have to collect them and are therefore inconsistent in their replies. A second reason might be that we used the words coupons and voucher instead of only one word and through that may have caused confusions.

4.2.4 Loyalty Cards
(Questions 11-13, see appendix B)

For enterprises, loyalty cards are a welcome promotion tool to bind customers as they work better than a series of independent promotion and give the companies the opportunity to collect customer's addresses for a more efficient direct advertising.[61] To find out about the influence of loyalty cards on shopping behaviour we planted a series of questions starting with the possession and possible influences on the store choice (n°12). Out of all replies we could detect the **ownership** of a loyalty-card in 59.4% (280 people). This percentage turned out to be significantly higher for women than for men. (women 67.9%, men 47.7% see filter). However, it only **influences** 6 out of 280 persons always in their shop-decision. 50 are often, 90 sometimes, 70 seldom and even 64 persons are never influenced by their loyalty card when it comes to selecting the store. That the results tend more to the non-influence of the cards might be due to the overload of these cards nowadays. People get confused and sometimes forget in which shops they are registered as clients; hence the influence of the shop choice is rather small.

For the reasons of influence we provided four factors, as shown in figure 8, and wanted to know the importance that each one has for the decision of the location. **Collecting bonus-points** was considered as important by almost half of the respondents. A mayor part of our sample (47.3%) regards **direct price advantages** through the card as an important reason, but also 15.6% think that they are rather or even not at all unimportant for the store-choice. To **redeem coupons** was also an important factor for 38.2% of the population. One third has a neutral opinion on a **favoured treatment** in the store and even 26.3% see it as a „not at all important" criterion for the selection of a store on the basis of a loyalty-card.

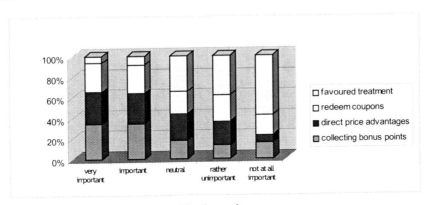

Figure 8: Question 13 – Reasons for usage of loyalty cards

As we see above, within the group of people using loyalty cards actively, the card has influence on the store choice because it provides more convenience for customer in terms of direct price advantages and coupons. The bad results for customer treatment could have two reasons. Either people really do not see it as important for the choice of their store, or they consider it as "not at all important" because they think that the cards do not have an effect on a favoured treatment.

---

[61] Lewis M., The Influence of Loyalty Programs and Short-term Promotions on Customer Retention

4.2.5 Sweepstakes

(Questions 21-24, see appendix B)

In respect to the sweepstakes we wanted to investigate if they represent an effective tool to create brand-awareness or if they are only seen as entertaining. Therefore, we asked in how many sweepstakes people had participated during the last year (n° 21) and if they did so, to state the company (n° 22) as well as possible changes in their attitude towards it (n° 23 & 24). Half of the respondents did not participate, 33.1% took part in 1-2 sweepstakes and 11.5% in 3-5. Only 27 persons out of 471 tried their luck more than five times.

The following results are sobering: **more than 80% cannot remember the company**. Within the little group of 19.1% of the interviewees that could remember dominated two kinds of sweepstake organisers. Newspapers and journals on the one hand like Bild, Stern and some women's magazines, and on the other hand tour operators and airlines like Germanwings, HLX or Thomas Cook. We can deduct that sweepstakes inside shops and supermarkets do not work well to improve a company's image as people forget about the brand. Maybe it is due to the shopping stress – people are more relaxed when sitting at home reading a newspaper or surfing in the Internet, they easier remember the company.

A vast majority of 84.3% has not changed their opinion on the company and voted for "neutral". Only 7 persons see the company more positive and 11 even more negative. In order to find out the reasons for a possible change in the opinion towards a company, we gave four closed answer possibilities (great/poor price, did win/did not win) and one field to state other reasons than the provided ones. Only seven persons out of our respondents won a prize (n° 24) although 237 (50.3%) participated in at least one sweepstake. In the "other" option we obtained the following responses: 19% complain that this kind of promotion just has the purpose of getting addresses for marketing activities afterwards; further 19% quote that a sweepstake has no influence on the image, as it is e.g. "no category of evaluating a company". 14.3% indicate that they do not expect to win anyway and one participant even calls it "a waste of time". Only two persons think the arranging companies "at least do something" and "show commitment".

As a result, sweepstakes obviously do not create brand-awareness in the majority of the cases. This means when people do not remember the brand or the company they will not buy the product due to participating in it and there will be no changes in the company's image. The only good thing from a company point of view might be the collection of addresses, but even this aim has already been seen through by a lot consumers and may fail as nearly every second rates direct mailing as annoying (see results n°14).

4.2.6 Customer's preferences

(Questions 25 & 26, see appendix B)

In order to summarize this part on the effectiveness of promotion tools we would like to reveal the outcomes of our question towards consumer's promotion preferences. The respondents were asked to develop a **ranking** from one to five for the promotion tools we are analysing. The results were allocated as the following table shows:

Rank	Tool	
1	Coupons/vouchers	1.78
2	Samples	2.17
3	Loyalty points/premiums	3.24
4	Loyalty cards	3.51
5	Sweepstakes	4.31

Figure 9: Question 25 – Ranking of promotion tools

On rank one we can find coupons/vouchers with an average score of 1.78, followed by samples. Position three is hard-fought by loyalty cards and loyalty points (representing the premium), whereby the points rank slightly higher with 3.24 before the cards with 3.51. The less favourite tool is the sweepstake.

In the last question (n°26) we gave the participants the possibility to state what they consider as wishful marketing or promotion activities. We can figure out three strong tendencies:

1. People want **free trials**, whereby some would like it to find them in their letterbox while others would prefer them at the point of sale. One participant states that he or she would prefer self-accessible trials in the stores so that you do not feel thronged. Another one would like the possibility to evaluate samples.
2. Our participants wish for more **objective and honest information** about products like technical details, the country where it was produced or specific information why brands are more expensive (e.g. "certificate dolphin-friendly fishing" for tuna). Some people complain about advertising stamped with stereotypes or cheating of different prices for different package sizes.
3. Many respondents desire a **reward of loyalty** or a more intensive **connection** between the promotion programmes of distinct companies. Others would appreciate a good service for example regarding consulting, delivery or after-sales. People wish for trained personnel at the point of sale who is able to provide the customer with the information requested but without being rushed.

Furthermore, people are looking for spontaneous, creative activities. They would like humorous promotion like the British Kit Kat packaging saying "remember you're not a salmon". One even mentioned the word "guerrilla" because "it is difficult to perceive promotion due to the overkill". Guerrilla Marketing is unconventional and intents to get maximum results from minimal resources.[62] In addition, our respondents want intelligent slogans and independent product comparisons like "Stiftung Warentest". Several persons mention the "buy two-get one free" system, which is not common in Germany. Eventually, people prefer useful promotional gifts like "rechargeable lighters" to "key chains".

---

[62] http://www.marketingterms.com/dictionary/guerilla_marketing/

4.3 Effects on the decision-making process

Now that we know about people's general attitude towards the single promotion tools, we can apply them according to each step of the purchase decision-making process. It is important for entrepreneurs to know about people's feelings, hopes, fears and expectations to implement these techniques in the correct manner. The results of our survey, more precisely how the promotion tools influence the customer, will be analysed in the following to give a support for marketing departments.

4.3.1 Problem/Need recognition

(Questions 1, 4, 14, 18, see appendix B)
According to the different causes of the problem recognition, the marketing department has to act in different ways. If a company launches a product or new brand samples should be distributed, as the reason that it is a new product is often the determining incentive to pick up a trial (question n°4). To investigate this issue more in detail we asked our participants if they usually search for new products or if they prefer to stay with the already known. The results are quite equated. 4.5% are always on the run for innovations and 3.4% never are. While 20.8% often look for them, 24.0% seldom do it. 223 of 471 respondents say that they are sometimes in search for new products (n°18). The answers of question one and two support this data: more than 63% consider their shopping habits as important or very important. As not everyone actively searches for new products, the marketing department has to show commitment in handing out free trials to create awareness of the product.

Attentiveness can also be produced by **direct mailing**. Nevertheless, question 14 reveals the risk of backfiring. We asked our participants how they evaluate the receipt of advertising from companies where they are registered as clients. The results are demonstrated in figure 10. It is remarkable that 44.1% find it annoying. One quarter consider it as informative and 14.0% as advantageous while 13.4% do not care. 4.3% are not registered as clients of any company; hence they fall out of the possible target of mailing activities.

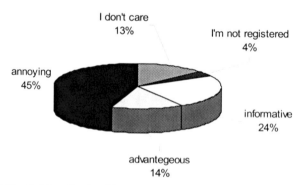

Figure 10: Question 14 – Opinion direct mailing

If the need emerges because the product has run out at home, coupons can be implemented to achieve a higher or faster repurchase. The same tool could help to stimulate the purchase of related products (Buy our coffee machine – get 10% off Melitta coffee filters).

4.3.2 Information search
(Questions 1, 3, 15, see appendix B)

During this stage, the marketing department should provide the consumer with all necessary information to convince him of the product. This can amongst others be done on one hand by offering him the possibility to test the product and on the other one by providing him with information about special promotion like coupons. However, it seems not very important to the populace to taste food like snacks, sauces or soups before purchasing them (n°3). It is rather stated as important for non-edible articles, probably due to higher prices and a longer product life.

Nevertheless, it could be important to provide the consumer with at least the possibility to get a food sample, as 97.5% of the respondents evaluated the criterion "taste" as a reason for purchase with "important" or even "very important" (n° 1). Furthermore, 33.4% chose these two options for the importance of testing drinks and 28.3% for the field of cold cuts like cheese or sausage (n°3). Often people do not buy certain products, as they fear to be disappointed with the purchase. For the company it is advantageous if the customer tries the product – although he may dislike it and does not buy it – because then the company has the guarantee that those consumers who buy it are all satisfied, spread good word-of-mouth and probably repurchase the item.

A good possibility to stimulate consumption is the emission of coupons. As more than half of the participants are interested in collecting and redeeming them (n° 15), it could be considered as useful tool to provide the customer with information about e.g. price reductions in advance, which could have positive effects on the evaluation of alternatives.

4.3.3 Evaluating alternatives
(Questions 5, 9, 10, 16, see appendix B)

After having tried a sample, the consumer interprets the information received and forms an attitude towards the product. If the trial is evaluated positively the item will be incorporated in his evoked set. As only 17.6% seldom or never purchase a product after having received a sample, there is a big opportunity to generate sales in the case of the remaining 82.4% (n° 5).

In case of **brand loyalty**, the evoked set is very small and other brands have hardly a chance to be considered as possible purchase option. To detect people's brand loyalty, we posed questions nine and ten regarding Coca-Cola and Pepsi, because we made the experience of strong loyalty concerning these two brands. The respondents were questioned which brand they prefer and if they would buy the corresponding other brand if it was especially promoted. Out of the two brands 65.0% chose Coca-Cola, 6.8% voted for Pepsi and 28.2% were indecisive. In total we found out that a majority of 39.7% never buys the other product when it is on offer, while 5.5% always do it (see figure 11).

It was interesting to see that half of the **Coca-Cola** drinkers never buy **Pepsi**, while only 15.6% of the Pepsi drinkers would never decide for Coca-Cola (see filter n° 10). We can conclude that Coca-Cola drinkers are more brand loyal than Pepsi clients. This might be because in Germany Coca-Cola is sold in most of the bars and restaurants; hence Pepsi consumers are used to change the brand frequently.

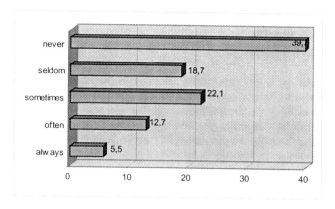

Figure 11: Question 10 – I buy the promoted, other brand

Besides the brand name the **price** is an essential criterion for evaluating alternative products. Therefore we wanted to know whether people usually compare prices. 65.4% of the respondents admit doing so always or often, just 11.0% say that they seldom or never do it. The remainder sometimes compares them. As many high quality products are sold at a high price, a promotional campaign stating a price reduction can help to gain the attention of shoppers who put emphasis on comparing prices when coming to a purchase decision.

4.3.4 Making the decision
(Questions 1, 2, 12, 13, 20, 26, see appendix B)

After having evaluated the different alternatives in advance, the establishment has to be selected. To influence in the choice of the shop companies implement customer **loyalty cards**, although our results reveal that only 11.9% are often or always influenced by this card in the store-selection (n°12). Another way of rewarding loyalty is the collection of fidelity points to receive a gift, which can lead the consumer to decide for the product of a certain enterprise.

Once in the store, the decision is influenced by e.g. in-store promotion activities, packaging and the personnel. To get a general overview which criteria are really important to the consumer when coming to a purchase decision concerning food and hygiene/cosmetic products, we put questions one and two. The five answer possibilities ranged from "very important" to "not at all important".

For **food** products we can see that the **price** is important to 63.1% and very important to 22.7%, while the **quality** of a product is very important to 43.7% and important to 50.7%. Only one person states the price and nobody the quality as not at all important. Not surprisingly, the **taste** of edibles is very important to the majority of the respondents (66.9%), followed by 30.6% who consider it as important.

In general, the answers show a neutral or rather unimportant view on the **packaging**. Nevertheless, we could find a difference between the male and the female results: 17.9% of the women regard it as important compared to men with 10.2%. As figure 12 shows, even 37.1% of the male respondents see it as rather unimportant. This tendency should be considered by companies while designing their packaging.

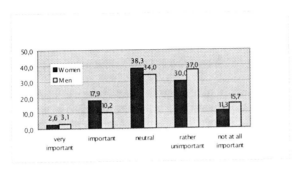

Figure 12: Question 1 – Packaging

Two further criteria for this question were **brands** and offers. The brands of food products seem to be "rather unimportant" to more than one third of the respondents. Another third has a neutral view on this matter. Here, we could detect that men put slightly more importance to brands than women (figure 13). This confirms the DPM brand loyalty study conducted in Germany recently.

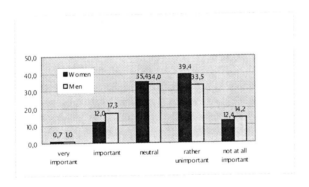

Figure 13: Question 1 – Brands

47.4% of our sample evaluate **offers** as important and 14.0% even as very important. Only 7.7% consider them as rather or completely unimportant. We can deduct that products, which are never especially promoted, will have it difficult to survive on the long run as customers expect promotion activities.

Considering the **hygiene or cosmetic** products we could find almost the same allocation of the results as above mentioned. Slight differences could be discovered for the quality yet that it is seen as very important by 3 percent points more. In this product group women lay more emphasis on quality than men. While 53.3% of the female state it as very important only

37.1% of the male do so. Similar responses were given for the smell of a product as "very important" was chosen by 9 percent points more by women than by men. These results were quite expected since women in general use more cosmetic products as for example make-up.

Building up on these questions, we posed number 20 asking which is the determining factor to **select a product** out of two equal ones. The predominant majority of 79.4% voted for the one with the more favourable price and only a very small group saw the premium as an incentive for purchase. 11.9% decided in favour for the product of their preferred brand. These results might be due to the income level as more than half of the participants dispose of less than 1,000€ a month. We see that the financial status still influences in the deal proneness.

To investigate the brand loyalty a bit deeper we filtered the participants who decided for the **brand** product. We could confirm a stronger tendency to brands at the men's side with 14.7% compared to only 9.9% at the women's side, which again supports the German brand loyalty study. In general, the subgroup of brand-buyers lays stronger emphasis on the importance of quality than the average (96.5% in question 1, ∅ 94.4%). While 63.5% of all participants consider offers as very important or important, only 35.7% of this subgroup think in this way. This affirms the quotation of quality conscious shoppers not being very prone to price promotions. In addition, we could find out that the statement of former research concerning the increase of brand loyalty with a higher net-income is true.

Furthermore, the results of question 26 approve the importance of qualified and discreet **personnel**. Thus, companies should invest in their staff to ensure a customer-friendly treatment, which might be a problem in low price supermarkets working with many people on a part-time basis and receiving little wages. Here, the relationship marketing approach has to ensure proper selection and training of employees.

4.3.5 Post-purchase evaluation
(Questions 14, 16, 17, see appendix B)

Promotion is a good opportunity to improve the post-purchase state of the consumer. Trying samples decreases the probability of buying a product that does not meet our expectations. Coupons and other price reductions lessen the feeling of dissatisfaction in case that the product does not convince the customer. At least you did not pay the whole price! A positive rating means the product is taken in the evoked set and increases the likelihood of repurchase. Once that the customer has retained it in his set, he will be more attentive for advertising of this brand.

For further investigation about price sensitivity, we asked our participants if they get annoyed when they **find a recently bought product at a more favourable price** in another store (n°17). Only 6.8% of the respondents do not care at all. 41.2% get very annoyed and more than half of the persons told us that it displeases them. Filtering the group of people getting very annoyed, we surprisingly found out that almost 70 % of this subgroup are women. In general, nearly half of the female respondents are very annoyed when they see a product cheaper elsewhere, while only 29.9% of the men chose this option. One tenth of the male part does not care at all, on the women's side it is just one twentieth.

Furthermore, we could detect that all persons who dislike finding products cheaper elsewhere ("very annoyed") have a more positive attitude to direct advertising activities (n°14). 28.1% (∅ 24.2%) evaluate it as informative and 16.1% (∅ 14.0%) as advantageous. The percentage concerning the comparison of prices is also higher with 80.9% stating that they always or often do it. Figure 14 demonstrates the apportionment of the outcomes: blue = "very annoyed", red = average.

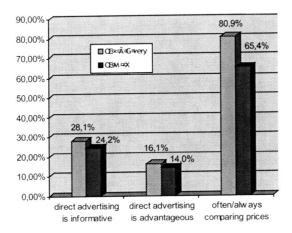

Figure 14: Question 17 – Filter for very annoyed

To conclude, we could observe that the theory concerning samples and coupons seems right with their statements as people seem to like and use them, but premiums and sweepstakes in contrast perform worse than formerly indicated as the excitement is often missing and the effort to gain a price is too high or the probability too low. Loyalty cards as an attempt to bind customers seem to work only partly and demand improvements for a more intense usage. The resulting conclusions for marketing strategies will be discussed in the following chapter.

5 Discussion

In the following we will transfer our results to the practice and point out what they signify for firms' marketing execution. Further, we shall give answers to each of our three research questions.

5.1 Consequences for companies

It is crucial for companies to know customers' general attitudes and reactions towards sales promotion methods so as to apply suitable methods to raise their attention as well as interest for a product, provoke the desire and action to buy it and through this secure their own profit and survival. Therefore, the consequences of consumer behaviour are going to be discussed in detail as follows.

5.1.1 General attitudes

In the introduction and the theory part about sales promotion we quoted that companies are shifting their marketing budget from advertising to sales promotion activities. Our results support this change as the majority of our respondents consider offers as an important criterion when coming to a purchase decision, while they see advertisements mailed directly to them as annoying. Nevertheless, entrepreneurs should be aware of customer's preferences as well as life styles in order to implement the single tools effectively.

Many consumers consider their shopping habits as important, so the evoked set is rather tight. We think this could be partly due to the increasing time-lack of people as it is usual nowadays that all members of a household have full-time jobs. Hence, **companies should lay stronger emphasis on in-store promotion activities**, which shorten the time to come to a decision and might also successfully interfere in the habit by making them buy another product than usually.

In case of brand loyalty the evoked set is also very small. We wanted to find out if brand-loyal customers switch to other trademarks only because they are especially promoted. The Coca-Cola and Pepsi example indicates that it depends on the brand, as Coca-Cola drinkers are more loyal than Pepsi ones. Sure that it is more difficult to attract brand-loyal consumers, but it is not impossible as seen in the cola example. **Once achieved that a formerly loyal customer switched to another brand, it is also more likely that he will frequently buy the new one**. Furthermore, we could confirm that brand loyalty grows together with the income, but as more than half of our respondents dispose of less than 1,000€ a month, the answers in general tended more to price consciousness than brand loyalty.

This low-income structure could also be the reason why offers in general are evaluated as important when coming to a purchase decision. People with financial constraints are more prone to promotion activities. At this point we see a pressure for companies as one can notice the growing tendency in Germany to shop in outlet-stores or low-cost supermarkets like Aldi or Lidl. People are not necessarily willing to pay a high price for a product which they could buy cheaper elsewhere. However, those participants, who see quality as a significant criterion for a purchase, might not trust in the cheap range of products of the low-cost supermarkets. The heuristic that quality has to have a certain price dominates. Therefore material incentives have to be implemented to gain the customer in the ordinary establishments. **One promotion**

instrument wished for by our respondents was "buy two – get one free", which could increase brand loyalty when people are using a product for a long time (twice as long) and they are satisfied with it. The extended usage can convert into a habit and might integrate the product into everyday life.

Furthermore, it often makes sense to distinguish between a male and female target to launch new products successfully. The target group for example influences in the packaging. We found out that **women set more value on packaging than men**. Hence, the wrapping should be more attractive for e.g. low-fat products as usually more female consumers purchase them. Sometimes companies just modify existing products to reach another audience. As we can observe a tendency to metro sexuality of men in the last few years, the male population will probably lay more importance on hygiene and cosmetic products in future. Companies like Nivea are going the right way with launching an anti-wrinkle cream especially for men, which is packed in blue carton instead of white for the female range. In addition, we saw that **among the owners of loyalty cards dominate the women**; so companies could direct their marketing strategies more accordant to female likings, e.g. give out cards in an appealing design.

In general, people are looking for honest information concerning products. They do not want to feel fooled by the manufacturer. Companies have already made an attempt to provide the customer with more information by establishing telephone hotlines or web pages. Nevertheless, it is not very probable that someone calls the hotline from the store before purchasing the product. **More data about the product should be printed on the packaging and competent staff should be available**. Many respondents complain about dull personnel, which is neither willed nor able to provide them with the information desired. Additionally, we can figure out the desire to get honoured among material and financial incentives of promotion. **True clients want to be rewarded** e.g. by price reductions – directly, at the end of a certain period or in form of vouchers – or by attractive premiums. We see that the relationship approach, which lays more emphasis on personal relations through capable employees as well as honouring loyal consumption, is the right technique to gain and retain customers.

5.1.2 Attitudes towards promotion

Our results show that some tools, like samples or loyalty cards, exert an influence on customers' shopping behaviour, while others like sweepstakes or premiums do not seem to have the wanted effects. Building up on the results, each tool will now be taken into a critical consideration.

Regarding **free samples**, we wanted to investigate if people are really interested in the product or if they only take samples because they are for free. Although in the answer column "always" (in n°4) dominates the option "I take them because they are for free", we can observe that the majority also picks them up "often" because they are interested in taste/quality or in a new product. In addition, we learn from our last question that several people even wish for more samples in order to try products before buying them. If we combine these answers with the fact that one third always or often buys the product after having tried a sample, we can assume that samples are an efficient tool to arise interest and have an impact on the final purchase decision.

The tricky part with samples is their efficient distribution. It has to be considered carefully, when and where to hand them out to the target population. We found two good examples in this field: Nestlé handed out free trials of their instant coffee together with application tips to students as they had found out that most people convert to coffee drinkers in a full-time job.[63] We could imagine giving out chewing gum samples together with onion crisps or clothes-vouchers distributed with weight watchers products.

Another example comes from a Parisian advertising agency that distributed perfume samples in selected restaurants between the main course and the dessert.[64] This action embraced several advantages: first, the relaxed atmosphere during dinner was well chosen as you are normally in a better mood in a nice restaurant than in the shop. Second, you are not distracted from other perfume fragrances and last but not least you are prone to buy the fragrance if your partner likes the perfume. This type of marketing is called **Guerrilla Marketing** and was also mentioned on the "wish list" of our respondents.

It should also be taken into account *how* they can be handed out. To guarantee a trial right on the spot, beverage cans for example could be opened directly by the promoting personnel to avoid that the customer takes it but does not try it. We experienced this action in Spain on the way from the bus stop to the university, where suiting circumstances like heat and time were given. In a supermarket it could be rather bothering to carry an open can.

The intent to adapt to customers' changing life styles, namely distribute samples via Internet, is understandable but not always adequate. First, it seems not very popular to use the websites distributing them. Second, we see the risk of abuse in these pages, as probably those people who use them may exploit them, so that they e.g. always have shampoo for free. Due to the fact that within the results for the reasons of usage "I like surfing in the internet" and "I get something for free" rank before "I am interested in new products", we do not evaluate it as a successful medium to distribute innovations. A better idea would be the possibility to apply for a free sample directly on the home page of the manufacturer instead of selecting samples out of a huge range on online-company sites. Like this you can guarantee to a higher degree that people are really interested in the product and as well limit the number of samples sent to a household. A further advantage would be the receipt of customers' addresses combined with the knowledge about his interests.

We found out that **coupons** are the Germans' favourite promotion tool. However people do not seem to be very interested in cutting them out of magazines. In order to facilitate the use and the procedure of collecting, companies should consider the possibility to place coupons on the shelf next to the product. This has to be done very carefully though, as it would probably increase sales but could also nullify their biggest advantage by making them accessible to every person passing the shelf. With that the price reduction would not be limited to a certain target anymore.

To strengthen the repurchase, we advise the emission of coupons in the period after having distributed a sample. When people are convinced by it, they buy the product for the first time and simultaneously receive a voucher for the next purchase. Once started the chain of buying, the company could establish a fixed place in customers' evoked set. This double promotion probably cannot be implemented for low-price products as the charges for the samples and coupons might be too high.

Concerning **with-pack-premiums**, we could find out that they do not triumph within the population interviewed. This may be due to the circumstances that no people under 17 years

---

[63] http://www.marketing.de/artikel/?cat=2&id=123
[64] http://www.guerilla-marketing-blog.de/CommentView,guid,3d0f89ca-aa9b-4d5c-83ef-2e70cc57d371.aspx

participated. It is namely difficult to find adequate and attractive gifts for adults, whereas children are easier to allure with e.g. little toys or stickers. We see a big opportunity in implanting these premiums in the children's market as attitudes towards brands can be formed already at an early age and the kids can be retained at as customers later on. Additionally, children use to exert influence on the decision-maker during the shopping trip. Although they do not dispose of own money, they often make their parents buy the products they want and are therefore a good target for marketing actions.

The **free-in-the-mail-premium**, in contrary to the with-pack-premium, might give more stimuli for adults, as it is easier to send reasonable gifts by mail than attaching them to a product. Also this method enforces repurchase, as a certain number of items has to be bought in order to obtain the required fidelity points. One respondent for example stated that he would like a company to combine their product with a tricot for the football world cup in 2006 so that everyone could afford to have one for the feeling of togetherness during the event. Another desirable with-pack-premium stated was the distribution of lotto-tickets, which are probably not suited for food products as the costs for the tickets would be too high.

Moreover, we had the aim to find out about a connection between short-and-long-term marketing tools i.e. sales promotion and relationship marketing. One of the first attempts to bind the customer was the release of customer **loyalty cards**, which combines several promotion tools. However, we can see that only 12% are often or always influenced by this card in the store-selection, thus the marketing department should either think of higher incentives to use them or to integrate more companies in one card system so that clients carry less cards but have more possibilities to obtain price reductions or bonus-points. This leads us to a new form of establishing a connection to the customer. As it is more difficult for commodity product providers to establish this relation, they should try to associate with non-commodity product distributors. The German payback system for example combines the supermarket chain *Real* with the hotel chain *nh hoteles* and *europcar* car rental. In other countries like Spain or Australia, as our respondents stated, one can find supermarkets giving a discount on petrol at certain gas stations.

A further model of rewarding loyalty can be found in a supermarket chain in Spain. The card obtained is smaller than usual ones and can be put on a key ring. In the shop distinct price labels are to be found, indicating a lower price for members. At the cash point, the client gets a price reduction on showing the card on the one hand, and on the other one he receives some coupons printed together with the receipt. There are no direct mailings and the customer decides if and when he wants to use the card without being harassed by advertising – which costs the company a lot of money and at the end only annoys the customer. Furthermore he gets more coupons the more often he shops at the supermarket. Client's loyalty is directly honoured without having to collect points. We consider this method as an intelligent and a pleasant way of binding the customer without running the risk of molesting him.

As already stated in the analysis, **sweepstakes** do not fulfil the aim of creating brand-awareness, since the majority of our respondents could not remember the organising firm. This promotion tool only seems to be useful to increase the fun-factor of the shopping trip but not to provoke a purchase of a special product. In some cases, it might even have a negative effect on the company image, yet that people know that it is often just a method to collect addresses for direct advertising.

Although we did not question the effects of contests because we assumed that the participation rate would be even lower than the one of sweepstakes, we could imagine that they have a higher impact on the creation of brand-awareness. Often they appeal to the contestants' creativity asking them to invent a slogan or a logo for a new brand or product, which links them to the item or enterprise in an effective way. On top of that, the company can save money for hiring designers or ad writers.

5.2 Conclusion

In order to sum up our paper we shall now answer our research questions. Before doing so, it should be considered, that our results only pertain to the German market whereas in other countries different promotion tools might prevail.

5.2.1 Effectiveness and influences of sales promotion on the decision-making process

Attracting the customer effectively is a complex task and needs to take a lot of aspects into consideration to influence in every step of the purchase decision-making process. A problem is also that companies have to meet the expectations of a broad mass without loosing the focus for their own profit. As it is often difficult to determine one single target group, it can be recommendable to target one single promotion action to different audiences in distinctive establishments by altered handling of distribution.

Regarding the single tools, the results for **samples** and **coupons** show us that if companies achieve to draw attention to their product within the first three steps of the purchase decision-making process, the likelihood of adding a product to the customer's evoked set and a final purchase, step four, will increase. The implementation of these two instruments can also have a positive impact on the post-purchase evaluation: samples provide the consumer with a true image of a product; hence the purchase after a trial will probably lead to a satisfaction.

Premiums and **loyalty cards** lay stronger emphasis on step three and four, the evaluation of alternatives and the purchase decision, as they reward the client for his loyalty and not necessarily provoke interest in a product or provide information about it. The influence of **sweepstakes** is relatively low; they rather try to improve the company's image. It may influence in the moment of coming to a purchase decision if customers participate in a sweepstake of a product standing on their shopping list. They do neither influence in steps one to three nor in step five.

Concerning the moment of selecting an article, it is not so much the material but rather the financial incentive in form of in-store price promotions that are able to change peoples' buying decisions. Repurchase, as a result of promotion, is tricky to measure but can be done by loyalty cards and points. Especially through the digital processing of information in case of the cards we can easily measure the product, the moment, the quantity and the frequency of purchase.

We found out that **especially the implementation of samples and coupons is highly recommendable.** Loyalty cards and premiums may need some reformation, but the customers still seem to make use of them. Sweepstakes do not provide the promised excitement, at least not in Germany. Despite the fact that most of the traditional tools still do their job, they seem to lose some of their effectiveness in the stimuli saturated world. As customers are bombarded with advertising, they no longer make an effort to read every flyer or coupon they find in their post box or the newspaper. Hence, the marketing department has to think twice how and through which tool they can arise interest as seen in the above-mentioned examples from

Nestlé and the Parisian advertising agency. Companies should be creative in the selection and implementation of the single promotion tools, and furthermore think about more possibilities to connect them as done by loyalty cards.

5.2.2 Is long-term customer relation appreciated?

As we are moreover living in days of hard competition, it is definitely recommendable to try to establish a relationship with the customer on the long run. But sales promotion is still necessary and the prerequisite to recruit primal customers to whom one can establish a relation later on. It is advisable to give consumers an incentive to try products, especially innovations, to arise interest in them. People even expect it. After that, companies can save money on re-attracting customers who are already loyal to their brand or shop by renouncing inadequate promotion tools as e.g. poor premiums in form of cheap XL-T-Shirts.

It might be more difficult for commodity product providers to create a bond, as it is not a personal relation between a vendor and a buyer but rather a relation between an establishment or a brand and the customer's attitude towards it. However, is not impossible as we could see in the results for loyalty cards mentioned above. In spite of being a sales promotion tool, they already indicate the tendency into a relationship with the customer on the long run. Nonetheless, **most of the current systems could be improved** to satisfy the customer according to his needs **and specially targeted advertising might have to be reconsidered as it is mostly seen as annoying**. We think that direct mailing in form of letters should preferably only be sent out on special occasions. Mailing activities via email can be executed more often as they are easier to get rid off, but should also only be distributed to inform about novelties or special offers that make you really appreciate the data provided as e.g. the announcement of special flight offers only valid on certain days.

A further important aspect for relationship building is the employment of friendly and helpful personnel, which is willed to get trained about the product or shop and so can be of assistance for the customer. This was desired by many of our respondents, hence companies should really lay emphasis on an adequate selection and training of employees to win and retain customers on the long run.

5.2.3 Combining sales promotion and relationship marketing

The possibility of combining these two marketing tools **depends on the product and its distribution channel**. As stated above, for commodity products it is more difficult to opt for customer relations than for industrial products or services yet that they are mostly distributed through a retailer. The manufacturer does not have much influence on the store personnel and is sometimes at the retailer's mercy when it comes to the execution of promotion action as he can refuse to cooperate.

We have seen though, that there are several promotion tools that are used to establish a connection between those two concepts. Above all, there are the **loyalty cards** in order to bind clients to certain stores or services. Also **free-in-the-mail premiums** stimulate repurchase and create a positive image of the company, which can contribute to a favourable attitude towards the emitting firm. Without a positive mind-set no value creation will take place. Sweepstakes and contests as well allude on improving the image of an enterprise but as seen above, their impact is not that high. Nevertheless, it can be used to collect data on customers' preferences and habits and herewith help the company to commit itself to the client.

5.2.4 Upshot

The conducted study reveals enlightening results concerning the German population and their sales promotion preferences. The reader could see that samples and coupons are the most popular tools, highly demanded and appreciated, whereby loyalty cards and points system need a slight improvement, but are still used by today's consumers. The loyalty programs and the sweepstakes or contests are common strategies linking short-and-long-term marketing methods. We see the concept of relationship marketing as necessary in days of high competition and influences in the purchase decision-making process, although not to the same degree as sales promotion does – at least not in the sector of commodity products.

Nevertheless, we obtained contradictory results concerning coupons, which might need further research in order to clarify the real effectiveness. Furthermore, former research articles stated that customers' financial situation does not have an impact on their deal proneness while others, including our research, confirm a dependency. This could be investigated in the future. In addition, we could imagine some research carried out by the distributor with the aim of measuring the success of sales promotion in single stores or within certain target groups. Samples could be combined with coupons, indicating a code of the distributing location. Through this, prospect promotion activities could be targeted more efficiently as companies would know better in which places which activities are suitable.

Finally, we can say that the art of gaining customers is to find the adequate promotion tool and to implement it efficiently, that means the costs of a promotion campaign should not be higher than the benefits achieved; whereby the art of retaining customers lies more in the hands of relationship marketing with the aim of providing the consumer with all service appreciated and desired. As we could see that the two investigated marketing concepts show connections, one cannot say which method is more recommendable. The art is to find the balance between these two approaches and an appropriate cost-benefit concept, with the aim to satisfy the customer to assure the maintenance of one's business in the market.

References

Literature

- **Belch, G. & M.**, Introduction to Advertising & Promotion, 1995, Irwin

- **Berná Pastor, N.**, Comportamiento del Consumidor, Universidad de Alicante, 2004/05

- **Hollensen, S.**, Global Marketing, A decision-oriented approach, 2004, Prentice Hall

- **Kotler, P.**, Marketing Management, 2000, Prentice Hall

- **Payne, A. et al.**, Relationship Marketing for Competitive Advantage, Winning and Keeping Customers, 1998, Butterworth-Heinemann

- **Persson, P.-G.**, Modeling the impact of Sales Promotion on store profits, 1995, Stockholm Scholl of Economics

- **Statt, David A.**, Understanding the Consumer, 1997, Macmillan Press LTD

- **Varey, R.**, Marketing Communication, Principles and Practice, 2002, Routledge

- **Zikmund, W. G.**, Business Research Methods, Sixth Edition, 2000, South-Western

Articles

- **Bawa K. and Shoemaker R.**, The Effects of Free Sample Promotions on Incremental Brand Sales, 2004, Marketing Science

- **Dpm-team**: Markentreue-Studie, 2004, W&V

- **Institut für Marktorientierte Unternehmensführung** (IMU): Effective Sales Promotion, 2004, W&V

- **Laroche et al.**, A model of consumer response to two retail sales promotion techniques, 2003, Elsevier Science Inc.

- **Lewis M.**, The Influence of Loyalty Programs and Short-term Promotions on Customer Retention, 2004, Journal of Marketing Research

- **Martinez and Montaner**, The effect of consumer's psychographic variables upon deal-proneness, 2005, Elsevier Science Inc.

- **Srinivasan, S., Anderson, R.;** Concepts and strategy guidelines for designing value enhancing sales promotions, 1998, Journal of Product & Brand Management

- **Wiesbadener Marketingberatung** UGW: POS-Marketing Report 2004, W&V

Internet sources

http://www.converge.on.ca

http://www.democratandchronicle.com

http://www.emerald-library.com

http://www.guerilla-marketing-blog.de

http://www.forschungsgruppe.de

http://www.managementhelp.org

http://www.marketing.de

http://www.marketingpower.com

http://www.marketingtoday.com

http://www.marketingterms.com

http://www.science-direct.com

http://en.wikipedia.org

Appendix A

I – Questionnaire (English version)

eonlinesurveys.com/rendersurvey.asp?id=132494

Page 1 of 8

Sales Promotion

Great that you dedicate some of your time to us!

Therefore, we will start straight away:

*1)

When buying food I select the products according to the following criteria

	very important	important	neutral	rather unimportant	not at all important
Price	○	○	○	○	○
Quality	○	○	○	○	○
Taste	○	○	○	○	○
Packaging	○	○	○	○	○
Brand-name	○	○	○	○	○
Offers	○	○	○	○	○
Habits	○	○	○	○	○

*2) When buying hygiene/cosmetic products I select the products according to the following criteria

	very important	important	neutral	rather unimportant	not at all important
Price	○	○	○	○	○
Quality	○	○	○	○	○
Smell	○	○	○	○	○
Packaging	○	○	○	○	○
Brand-name	○	○	○	○	○
Offers	○	○	○	○	○
Habits	○	○	○	○	○

I

Pre-test

^3)

How important is it for you to test the following products before purchasing them?

	very important	important	neutral	rather unimportant	not at all important
Snacks/Sweets	○	○	○	○	○
Yoghurt/Pudding	○	○	○	○	○
Soups/Dips	○	○	○	○	○
Cold cuts	○	○	○	○	○
Bakery	○	○	○	○	○
Drinks	○	○	○	○	○
Hygiene/Cosmetic products	○	○	○	○	○
Software/Internet-provider	○	○	○	○	○
Newspapers/Magazines	○	○	○	○	○

Samples

^4) I pick up samples because...

	always	often	sometimes	seldom	never
I am interested in taste/quality	○	○	○	○	○
they are for free	○	○	○	○	○
it is a new product	○	○	○	○	○

^5) If a sample convinced me I will buy the product on the next demand

○ always
○ often
○ sometimes
○ seldom
○ never

Naechste Seite

Samples - websites

*6) Do you know websites that offer free samples? (e.g. kostenlos.de, probino.de, warenproben.ag)

○ yes
○ no (please continue with question 9, next page)

7) How often do you use these websites?

○ always
○ often
○ sometimes
○ seldom
○ never (please continue with question 9)

8)

Why do you use these pages? Please rank the reasons according to their importance (1 for the most important reason)

because I am interested in new products ⌄
due to convenience ⌄
because I like to surf in the Internet ⌄
because I get something for free ⌄

Brand loyalty

*9) Which brand do you prefer?

○ Coca-Cola
○ Pepsi
○ I don't care

10) I buy the corresponding other brand when it is especially promoted

○ always
○ often
○ sometimes
○ seldom
○ never

[Previous Page] [Naechste Seite]

Loyalty cards

*11) Do you possess a customer loyalty card? (e.g. Payback)

- ○ yes
- ○ no (please continue with question 14)

12) Does it influence you in the choice of your shopping location?

- ○ always
- ○ often
- ○ sometimes
- ○ seldom
- ○ never

13) If it does so, for which reasons?

	very important	important	neutral	rather unimportant	not at all important
collect bonus points	○	○	○	○	○
direct price advantages	○	○	○	○	○
redeem coupons	○	○	○	○	○
favoured treatment	○	○	○	○	○

Direct Advertising

14) How would you evaluate the receipt of direct advertising (via post or email) of companies where you are registered as a client?

- ○ informative
- ○ advantageous
- ○ annoying
- ○ don't care
- ○ I am not registered at any company

| Previous Page | Naechste Seite |

Attitudes

^15)

I am interested in cutting out, collecting and redeeming coupons.

- ○ very much
- ○ a little bit
- ○ not at all

^16) I catch myself comparing prices.

- ○ always
- ○ often
- ○ sometimes
- ○ seldom
- ○ never

^17)

It annoys me to find a recently bought product cheaper in another store

- ○ very much
- ○ a little bit
- ○ not at all

^18) I look for new products

- ○ always
- ○ often
- ○ sometimes
- ○ seldom
- ○ never

^19) I buy a newspaper/magazine because of the premium

- ○ always
- ○ often
- ○ sometimes
- ○ seldom
- ○ never

^20)

Out of two equivalent products I choose the one with the

- ○ premium
- ○ cheaper price
- ○ favourite brand-name

Sweepstakes

^21) In how many sweepstakes did you participate during the last year?

- ○ 0 (please continue with question 25)
- ○ 1-2
- ○ 3-5
- ○ >5

22) Of which company/ies?

- ○ I can't remember (please continue with question 25)
- ○ Company:
  [   ]

23) How do you see your attitude towards the company after the sweepstake?

- ○ much more positive
- ○ more positive
- ○ neutral
- ○ more negative
- ○ much more negative

24) Why?

- ○ great prize
- ○ I won
- ○ poor prize
- ○ I did not win
- ○ other:
  [   ]

[Previous Page] [Naechste Seite]

Preferences

*25)

Please rank the following promotion tools according to your preferences (1 for your favourite)

free samples	▾
loyalty-cards	▾
coupons/voucher	▾
premiums	▾
sweepstakes	▾

26)

Would you wish for a certain promotion? Which? (optional)

[   ]

[Previous Page] [Naechste Seite]

Demographics

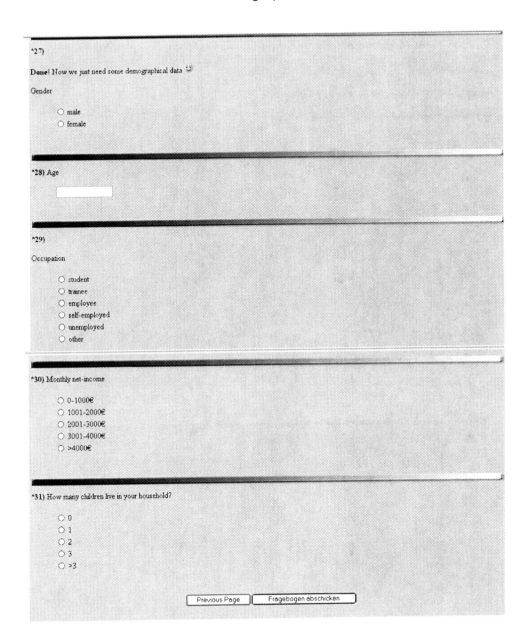

27)

Done! Now we just need some demographical data ☺

Gender

- ○ male
- ○ female

28) Age

[   ]

29)

Occupation

- ○ student
- ○ trainee
- ○ employee
- ○ self-employed
- ○ unemployed
- ○ other

30) Monthly net-income

- ○ 0-1000€
- ○ 1001-2000€
- ○ 2001-3000€
- ○ 3001-4000€
- ○ >4000€

31) How many children live in your household?

- ○ 0
- ○ 1
- ○ 2
- ○ 3
- ○ >3

[Previous Page] [Fragebogen abschicken]

II – Fragebogen (German version)

Sales Promotion

Schön, dass Sie uns ein wenig von Ihrer Zeit schenken!

Deswegen wollen wir auch gleich mit unseren Fragen loslegen:

Mittunivers
MID SWEDEN UNIV

*1) Beim Kauf von Lebensmitteln wähle ich nach folgenden Kriterien aus

	sehr wichtig	wichtig	neutral	eher unwichtig	völlig unwichtig
Preis	O	O	O	O	O
Qualität	O	O	O	O	O
Geschmack	O	O	O	O	O
Verpackung	O	O	O	O	O
Markenname	O	O	O	O	O
Angebote	O	O	O	O	O
Gewohnheit	O	O	O	O	O

*2) Beim Kauf von Hygiene-/Kosmetikprodukten wähle ich nach folgenden Kriterien aus

	sehr wichtig	wichtig	neutral	eher unwichtig	völlig unwichtig
Preis	O	O	O	O	O
Qualität	O	O	O	O	O
Geruch	O	O	O	O	O
Verpackung	O	O	O	O	O
Markenname	O	O	O	O	O
Angebote	O	O	O	O	O
Gewohnheit	O	O	O	O	O

Pre-Test

*3) Wie wichtig ist es für Sie die folgenden Produkte vor dem Kauf zu testen?

	sehr wichtig	wichtig	neutral	eher unwichtig	völlig unwichtig
Snacks/Süßigkeiten	○	○	○	○	○
Joghurt/Pudding	○	○	○	○	○
Suppen/Soßen	○	○	○	○	○
Aufschnitt	○	○	○	○	○
Backwaren	○	○	○	○	○
Getränke	○	○	○	○	○
Hygiene-/Kosmetikprodukte	○	○	○	○	○
Software/Internetanbieter	○	○	○	○	○
Zeitungen/Zeitschriften	○	○	○	○	○

Samples

*4) Ich nehme Produktproben mit weil...

	immer	oft	manchmal	selten	nie
ich interessiert an Qualität/Geschmack bin	○	○	○	○	○
sie gratis sind	○	○	○	○	○
es sich um neue Produkte handelt	○	○	○	○	○

*5) Wenn mich ein Pröbchen überzeugt hat, kaufe ich das Produkt beim nächsten Bedarf

○ immer
○ oft
○ manchmal
○ selten
○ nie

[Naechste Seite]

Samples - websites

*6) Kennen Sie Internetseiten die gratis Produktproben anbieten? (z.B. kostenlos.de, probino.de, warenproben.ag)

○ ja
○ nein (weiter zur Frage 9, nächste Seite)

7) Wie oft benutzen Sie diese Seiten?

○ immer
○ oft
○ manchmal
○ selten
○ nie (weiter zur Frage 9)

8)

Warum benutzen Sie diese Seiten? Ordnen Sie bitte die Gründe nach ihrer Wichtigkeit (1 entspricht dem wichtigsten Grund)

weil ich an Neuheiten interressiert bin ⌄
aus Bequemlichkeit ⌄
weil ich gerne im Internet surfe ⌄
weil ich etwas gratis bekomme ⌄

Brand loyalty

*9) Welche Marke bevozugen Sie?

○ Coca-Cola
○ Pepsi
○ ist mir egal

10) Ich kaufe die jeweils andere Marke, wenn sie im Angebot ist

○ immer
○ oft
○ manchmal
○ selten
○ nie

| Previous Page | Naechste Seite |

Loyalty Cards

^11) Besitzen Sie eine Kundenclub-Karte? (z.B. Payback)

- ○ ja
- ○ nein (weiter zur Frage 14)

12) Beeinflußt Sie diese in der Auswahl Ihres Geschäftslokals?

- ○ immer
- ○ oft
- ○ manchmal
- ○ selten
- ○ nie

13) Wenn es Sie beeinflußt, aus welchen Gründen?

	sehr wichtig	wichtig	neutral	eher unwichtig	völlig unwichtig
Punkte sammeln	○	○	○	○	○
direkte Preisvorteile	○	○	○	○	○
Coupons einlösen	○	○	○	○	○
bevorzugte Behandlung	○	○	○	○	○

Direct mailing

14) Wie beurteilen Sie den Erhalt von Werbung (per Post oder Email) von Firmen bei denen Sie als Kunde registriert sind?

- ○ informativ
- ○ Vorteil verschaffend
- ○ lästig
- ○ egal
- ○ ich bin bei keiner Firma registriert

[Previous Page] [Naechste Seite]

Attitudes

^15)

Ich bin daran interessiert Coupons auszuschneiden, zu sammeln und einzulösen.

- ○ sehr
- ○ ein wenig
- ○ gar nicht

^16) Ich erwische mich dabei, wie ich Preise vergleiche

- ○ immer
- ○ oft
- ○ manchmal
- ○ selten
- ○ nie

^17) Es ärgert mich, wenn ich ein kürzlich gekauftes Produkt in einem anderen Geschäft billiger sehe

- ○ sehr
- ○ ein wenig
- ○ gar nicht

^18) Ich suche nach neuen Produkten

- ○ immer
- ○ oft
- ○ manchmal
- ○ selten
- ○ nie

^19) Ich kaufe eine Zeitung/Zeitschrift wegen des Extras/der Beilage

- ○ immer
- ○ oft
- ○ manchmal
- ○ selten
- ○ nie

^20) Aus zwei gleichwertigen Produkten wähle ich das mit

- ○ der Gratisbeilage
- ○ dem günstigeren Preis
- ○ dem bevorzugten Markennamen

Sweepstakes

*21) An wie vielen Preisausschreiben haben Sie im letzten Jahr teilgenommen?

- ○ 0 (weiter zur Frage 25)
- ○ 1-2
- ○ 3-5
- ○ >5

22) Bei welcher Firma/welchen Firmen?

- ○ kann mich nicht erinnern (weiter zur Frage 25)
- ○ Unternehmen:

23) Wie sehen Sie die Firma/Firmen nach dem Preisausschreiben?

- ○ viel positiver
- ○ positiver
- ○ neutral
- ○ negativer
- ○ viel negativer

24) Warum?

- ○ toller Gewinn
- ○ ich habe etwas gewonnen
- ○ schlechter Gewinn
- ○ ich habe nichts gewonnen
- ○ Sonstiges

Preferences

*25)

Bitte ordnen Sie die folgenden verkaufsfördernden Maßnahmen gemäß Ihren Vorlieben (1 für die beliebteste)

Produktproben	▾
Kundenclub-Karten	▾
Coupons/Gutscheine	▾
Treuepunkte	▾
Preisausschreiben	▾

26)

Würden Sie sich eine bestimmte Marketingmaßnahme wünschen? Welche? (optional)

[Previous Page] [Naechste Seite]

Demographics

***27)**

Geschafft! Jetzt brauchen wir nur noch einige statistische Angaben ☺

Geschlecht

- ○ männlich
- ○ weiblich

*28) Alter

[   ]

*29)

Beruf

- ○ Student/in
- ○ Auszubildende/r
- ○ Angestellte/r
- ○ selbständig tätig
- ○ arbeitslos
- ○ anderer

*30) Monatliches Netto-Einkommen

- ○ 0-1000€
- ⊙ 1001-2000€
- ○ 2001-3000€
- ○ 3001-4000€
- ○ >4000€

*31) Wie viele Kinder leben in Ihrem Haushalt?

- ○ 0
- ○ 1
- ○ 2
- ○ 3
- ○ >3

[Previous Page] [Fragebogen abschicken]

Appendix B

I – Results

Results for: Sales Promotion

1) Beim Kauf von Lebensmitteln wähle ich nach folgenden Kriterien aus

	1 sehr wichtig	2 wichtig	3 neutral	4 eher unwichtig	5 völlig unwichtig	Responses	Average Score
Preis	107 (22.72%)	297 (63.06%)	51 (10.83%)	15 (3.18%)	1 (0.21%)	471	1.95 / 5 (39.00%)
Qualität	206 (43.74%)	239 (50.74%)	24 (5.10%)	2 (0.42%)	0 (0.00%)	471	1.62 / 5 (32.40%)
Geschmack	315 (66.88%)	144 (30.57%)	11 (2.34%)	1 (0.21%)	0 (0.00%)	471	1.36 / 5 (27.20%)
Verpackung	13 (2.76%)	69 (14.65%)	172 (36.52%)	155 (32.91%)	62 (13.16%)	471	3.39 / 5 (67.80%)
Markenname	4 (0.85%)	67 (14.23%)	164 (34.82%)	174 (36.94%)	62 (13.16%)	471	3.47 / 5 (69.40%)
Angebote	66 (14.01%)	223 (47.35%)	146 (31.00%)	30 (6.37%)	6 (1.27%)	471	2.34 / 5 (46.80%)
Gewohnheit	54 (11.46%)	245 (52.02%)	125 (26.54%)	36 (7.64%)	11 (2.34%)	471	2.37 / 5 (47.40%)
							2.36 / 5 (47.20%)

2) Beim Kauf von Hygiene-/Kosmetikprodukten wähle ich nach folgenden Kriterien aus

	1 sehr wichtig	2 wichtig	3 neutral	4 eher unwichtig	5 völlig unwichtig	Responses	Average Score
Preis	95 (20.17%)	248 (52.65%)	99 (21.02%)	27 (5.73%)	2 (0.42%)	471	2.14 / 5 (42.80%)
Qualität	219 (46.50%)	216 (45.86%)	33 (7.01%)	3 (0.64%)	0 (0.00%)	471	1.62 / 5 (32.40%)
Geruch	205 (43.52%)	196 (41.61%)	56 (11.89%)	12 (2.55%)	2 (0.42%)	471	1.75 / 5 (35.00%)
Verpackung	22 (4.67%)	75 (15.92%)	154 (32.70%)	174 (36.94%)	46 (9.77%)	471	3.31 / 5 (66.20%)
Markenname	33 (7.01%)	136 (28.87%)	139 (29.51%)	118 (25.05%)	45 (9.55%)	471	3.01 / 5 (60.20%)
Angebote	71 (15.07%)	202 (42.89%)	122 (25.90%)	60 (12.74%)	16 (3.40%)	471	2.46 / 5 (49.20%)
Gewohnheit	73 (15.50%)	224 (47.56%)	115 (24.42%)	46 (9.77%)	13 (2.76%)	471	2.37 / 5 (47.40%)
							2.38 / 5 (47.60%)

3) Wie wichtig ist es für Sie die folgenden Produkte vor dem Kauf zu testen?

	1 sehr wichtig	2 wichtig	3 neutral	4 eher unwichtig	5 völlig unwichtig	Responses	Average Score
Snacks/Süßigkeiten	11 (2.34%)	97 (20.59%)	147 (31.21%)	165 (35.03%)	51 (10.83%)	471	3.31 / 5 (66.20%)
Joghurt/Pudding	12 (2.55%)	87 (18.47%)	155 (32.91%)	174 (36.94%)	43 (9.13%)	471	3.32 / 5 (66.40%)
Suppen/Soßen	12 (2.55%)	72 (15.29%)	149 (31.63%)	187 (39.70%)	51 (10.83%)	471	3.41 / 5 (68.20%)
Aufschnitt	20 (4.25%)	113 (23.99%)	166 (35.24%)	133 (28.24%)	39 (8.28%)	471	3.12 / 5 (62.40%)
Backwaren	19 (4.03%)	95 (20.17%)	162 (34.39%)	157 (33.33%)	38 (8.07%)	471	3.21 / 5 (64.20%)
Getränke	24 (5.10%)	133 (28.24%)	145 (30.79%)	133 (28.24%)	36 (7.64%)	471	3.05 / 5 (61.00%)
Hygiene-/Kosmetikprodukte	72 (15.29%)	184 (39.07%)	111 (23.57%)	76 (16.14%)	28 (5.94%)	471	2.58 / 5 (51.60%)
Software/Internetanbieter	110 (23.35%)	170 (36.09%)	114 (24.20%)	52 (11.04%)	25 (5.31%)	471	2.39 / 5 (47.80%)
Zeitungen/Zeitschriften	75 (15.92%)	202 (42.89%)	102 (21.66%)	58 (12.31%)	34 (7.22%)	471	2.52 / 5 (50.40%)
							2.99 / 5 (59.80%)

4) Ich nehme Produktproben mit weil...

	1 immer	2 oft	3 manchmal	4 selten	5 nie	Responses	Average Score
ich interessiert an Qualität/Geschmack bin	78 (16.56%)	200 (42.46%)	124 (26.33%)	48 (10.19%)	21 (4.46%)	471	2.44 / 5 (48.80%)
sie gratis sind	130 (27.60%)	152 (32.27%)	105 (22.29%)	57 (12.10%)	27 (5.73%)	471	2.36 / 5 (47.20%)
es sich um neue Produkte handelt	75 (15.92%)	181 (38.43%)	131 (27.81%)	55 (11.68%)	29 (6.16%)	471	2.54 / 5 (50.80%)
							2.44 / 5 (48.80%)

5) Wenn mich ein Probchen überzeugt hat, kaufe ich das Produkt beim nächsten Bedarf

	Percentage	Responses
immer	2.1	10
oft	27.0	127
manchmal	53.3	251
selten	15.3	72
nie	2.3	11
Total responses:		471

14) Wie beurteilen Sie den Erhalt von Werbung (per Post oder Email) von Firmen bei denen Sie als Kunde registriert sind?

	Percentage	Responses
informativ	24.2	112
Vorteil verschaffend	14.0	65
lästig	44.1	204
egal	13.4	62
ich bin bei keiner Firma registriert	4.3	20
Total responses:		463

15)
Ich bin daran interessiert Coupons auszuschneiden, zu sammeln und einzulösen.

	Percentage	Responses
sehr	5.5	26
ein wenig	49.3	232
gar nicht	45.2	213
Total responses:		471

16) Ich erwische mich dabei, wie ich Preise vergleiche

	Percentage	Responses
immer	24.4	115
oft	41.0	193
manchmal	23.6	111
selten	9.3	44
nie	1.7	8
Total responses:		471

17) Es ärgert mich, wenn ich ein kürzlich gekauftes Produkt in einem anderen Geschäft billiger sehe

	Percentage	Responses
sehr	41.2	194
ein wenig	52.0	245
gar nicht	6.8	32
Total responses:		471

18) Ich suche nach neuen Produkten

	Percentage	Responses
immer	4.5	21
oft	20.8	98
manchmal	47.3	223
selten	24.0	113
nie	3.4	16
Total responses:		471

19) Ich kaufe eine Zeitung/Zeitschrift wegen des Extras/der Beilage

	Percentage	Responses
immer	0.6	3
oft	5.7	27
manchmal	20.2	95
selten	33.8	159
nie	39.7	187
Total responses:		471

20) Aus zwei gleichwertigen Produkten wähle ich das mit

	Percentage	Responses
der Gratisbeilage	8.7	41
dem günstigeren Preis	79.4	374
dem bevorzugten Markennamen	11.9	56
Total responses:		471

21) An wie vielen Preisausschreiben haben Sie im letzten Jahr teilgenommen?

	Percentage	Responses
0 (weiter zur Frage 25)	49.7	234
1-2	33.1	156
3-5	11.5	54
>5	5.7	27
Total responses:		471

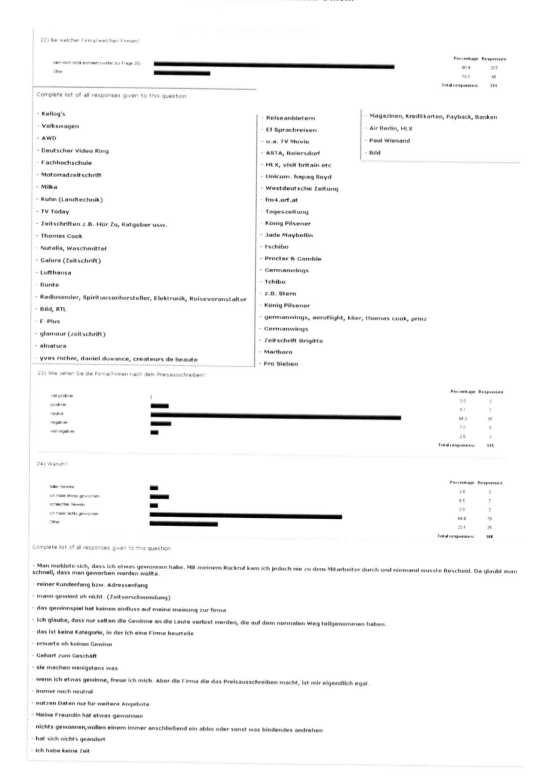

22) Bei welcher Firma/welchen Firmen?

	Percentage	Responses
kann mich nicht erinnern (weiter zur Frage 25)	80.9	203
Other	19.1	48
Total responses:		251

Complete list of all responses given to this question

- Kellog's
- Volkswagen
- AWD
- Deutscher Video Ring
- Fachhochschule
- Motorradzeitschrift
- Milka
- Kuhn (Landtechnik)
- TV Today
- Zeitschriften z.B. Hör Zu, Ratgeber usw.
- Thomas Cook
- Nutella, Waschmittel
- Galore (Zeitschrift)
- Lufthansa
- Bunte
- Radiosender, Spirituosenhersteller, Elektronik, Reiseveranstalter
- Bild, RTL
- E-Plus
- glamour (zeitschrift)
- alnatura
- yves rocher, daniel duvance, createurs de beaute

- Reiseanbietern
- Ef Sprachreisen
- u.a. TV Movie
- ASTA, Beiersdorf
- HLX, visit britain etc
- Unicum. hapag lloyd
- Westdeutsche Zeitung
- fm4.orf.at
- Tageszeitung
- König Pilsener
- Jade Maybellin
- tschibo
- Procter & Gamble
- Germanwings
- Tchibo
- z.B. Stern
- König Pilsener
- germanwings, aeroflight, klier, thomas cook, prinz
- Germanwings
- Zeitschrift Brigitte
- Marlboro
- Pro Sieben

- Magazinen, Kreditkarten, Payback, Banken
- Air Berlin, HLX
- Paul Wienand
- Bild

23) Wie sehen Sie die Firma/Firmen nach dem Preisausschreiben?

	Percentage	Responses
viel positiver	0.0	0
positiver	6.1	7
neutral	84.3	97
negativer	7.0	8
viel negativer	2.6	3
Total responses:		115

24) Warum?

	Percentage	Responses
toller Gewinn	2.8	3
ich habe etwas gewonnen	6.5	7
schlechter Gewinn	2.8	3
ich habe nichts gewonnen	64.8	70
Other	23.1	25
Total responses:		108

Complete list of all responses given to this question

- Man meldete sich, dass ich etwas gewonnen habe. Mit meinem Rückruf kam ich jedoch nie zu dem Mitarbeiter durch und niemand wusste Bescheid. Da glaubt man schnell, dass man geworben werden wollte.
- reiner Kundenfang bzw. Adressenfang
- mann gewinnt eh nicht. (Zeitverschwendung)
- das gewinnspiel hat keinen einfluss auf meine meinung zur firma
- Ich glaube, dass nur selten die Gewinne an die Leute verlost werden, die auf dem normalen Weg teilgenommen haben.
- das ist keine Kategorie, in der ich eine Firme beurteile
- erwarte eh keinen Gewinn
- Gehört zum Geschäft
- sie machen wenigstens was
- wenn ich etwas gewinne, freue ich mich. Aber die Firma die das Preisausschreiben macht, ist mir eigendlich egal.
- immer noch neutral
- nutzen Daten nur für weitere Angebote
- Meine Freundin hat etwas gewonnen
- nichts gewonnen,wollen einem immer anschließend ein abbo oder sonst was bindendes andrehen
- hat sich nichts geändert
- ich habe keine Zeit

- weil köpi immer noch herrlich schmeckt...

- Preisausschreiben aendern nichts am Image.

- nur mölichkeit adressen zu ziehen

- oft nur Versuch Neukunden zu locken

- Tun etwas für ihre Kunden, zeigen Engagement und verschaffen den Kunden Vorteile (Gewinnchancen)

- läuft noch

- Verlosung ist erst Ende Dezember

25)

Bitte ordnen Sie die folgenden verkaufsfördernden Maßnahmen gemäß Ihren Vorlieben (1 für die beliebteste)

		Average Score	Responses
Produktproben		2.17 / 5	471
Kundenclub-Karten		3.51 / 5	471
Coupons/Gutscheine		1.78 / 5	471
Treuepunkte		3.24 / 5	471
Preisausschreiben		4.31 / 5	471
		4.31 · 5	

26)

Wurden Sie sich eine bestimmte Marketingmaßnahme wünschen? Welche? (optional)

Complete list of all responses given to this question

- sinnvolle produktbeilagen

- mehr Warenproben

- nein

- Die Effizienz der großen Firmen und ihrer Marketingkommunikation durch ein aus der Markenwelt heraus entwickeltes Content-Feld im TV zu erhöhen, zB dem Kaffeeprodukt "Krönung light" ist der Aspekt "Selbstverwirklichung" herausgenommen worden und in ein bestehendes TV-Format, nämlich die Pro7-Sendung "Sam", integriert worden

- Zur kommenden Fußball-WM sollte sich jeder Interessierte zwecks Zusammengehörigkeitsgefühl ein Deutschland-Trikot leisten können. Da diese jedoch sehr teuer, würde ich es begrüßen, wenn eine Firma sie günstig ggf. in Kombination mit einem ihrer Produkte anbieten würde.

- 0

- nein

- mehr sachliche >Produktinformationen

- Rabatte/Geschenke bei guter Kundenverbindung und/oder best. Jahresumsatz

- Nein

- kostenlose Proben

- Alles, was neu ist, ist meist auch überflüssig. Die Kosten kann man sich sparen.

- Nonfood Geld zurück Garantie

- nein.

- nein

- geschultes Personal vor Ort
direkte Ansprache, Beratung
Kauf auf Probe

- Keine Musikberieselung

- Autonom zugängliche Produktproben, die sich im Bereich der VK-Ware befinden. So wird man nicht immer "dumm" angesprochen und kann sich in Ruhe entscheiden. Ich bin zwar sehr gut in der Lage " Nein" zu sagen, doch ich fühle mich gerne unbedrängt.

- individuellere Beratung ohne Kaufzwang

- konkrete Sachinformationen , z.B. technische Daten, Inhaltsstoffe , etc.

- Mehr Proben anfordern dürfen und dann auch (zur Not)Beurteilungen darüber schreiben und abgeben müssen

- Keine! Ich finde das Payback System sehr gut, es mußten aber noch mehr Partner dran teilnehmen.

- Marketingmaßnahme: Wunschgedanke Mehr Lohn und Preisstabilität zu gunsten der Enverbraucher;-)

- Tester - analog Testschläfer von IKEA

- nein

- Proben zusenden

- vernünftige Preise
keine "Verarschung" bei den Preisen zwischen Groß- und Normalpackungen

- Service

- zwei zum preis von einem

- Mehr Aktionen wie "buy two get one free". Vor allen Dingen bei Lebensmitteln. Nicht immer nur einfache Sonderangebote sondern Spezialaktionen womit der Kunde für sein Einkaufsverhalten belohnt wird.

- GUerillia - unerwartet, damit man es auch wahrnimmt bei dem ganzen Overkill

- eventuell mehr verkostungen. aber ansonsten nein, denn konsumenten werden zu genügend überflutet.

- nein

- keine ahnung

- Erweiterung des Miles and More Programmes auf Supermärkte, etc.

- mir fällt au anhieb keine ein

- Proben nach Hause...

- Produktproben im Handel

- Produktvergleiche wie bei Stiftung Warentest finde ich sehr gut

- aufklärend, ehrlich, informativ

- spezifische Information, warum dieses Markenprodukt teurer sein muss als andere, würde Kaufentscheidung bestimmt beeinflussen (z.B. "Fischfang delphinfreundlich" wie Oetker)

- möglichst überhaupt keine - da lästig

- keine

- Verkostung am POS, "Proben-Abonnement"

- Werbung die informativ ist, oder kluegere Sprueche (Geitz ist geil - kann man da noch flacher werden?)oder erfrischende, mit dem Produkt nicht relevante Sprueche. In GBR steht z.B auf der KitKat Verpackung "remember you're not a salmon". Einfach nur so... (gut genug, um in Erinnerung zu bleiben...)

- Mehr über das Produkt selbst zu erfahren.
z.B.: Wenn ich mir einen Pullover kaufe will ich wissen ob er in einem Billiglohnland hergestellt wurde oder nicht.

- keine

- Warengutschein bei Kauf eines Produktes, z.B. 5 Euro pro Hose bei einem Händler

- Sonderrabatte

- Die einzige Marketingmaßnahme die ich als wirklich sinnvoll erachte, ist diejenige dass mir das unternehmen vermittelt dass es stets an top-leistungen interessiert ist, d.h. wenn fehler und reklamationen auftreten, diese kundenfreundlich und kulant zu regeln. nur wenn ich den eindruck habe, dass auch dem antspr. unternehmen etwas daran liegt, seine leistung ordentlich und zuverlässig zu erbringen, bin ich bereit, diese produkte weiter zu konsumieren und das unternehmen zu unterstuetzen.

- teilweise intensivere und persönlichere Beratung (z.B. Kosmetikfirmen) --> meiner Meinung effektiv zur Kundengewinnung und -bindung, auch langfristig.

- nein

- Gute und nette Beratung und entspannende Einkaufsatmosphäre.

- nein, keine bestimmte

- Gratisproben nach Hause gesendet kriegen (kostenlos)

- mehr spontane, kreative aktionen

- Befragungen über das Produkt

- Mengenrabatte, sowas wie einen Stammkundenrabatt faende ich gut. Gibt's im Ausland oefter: "buy one, get one free"!

- Preis senken

- nein - gibt schon genug

- wenig aufdringlich aber leicht zugänglich durch hohe Präsenz

- Ich würde mir wünschen, daß Leute, die Produkte oder Proben anbieten, auch voll über das Produkt/Probe informiert sind; dementsprechend auf Fragen antworten können. Ich will nicht sehen, daß die Leute kein Bock oder keine Ahnung vom Produkt/Probe haben!

- pampers

- Praktische Werbeartikel, also keine Schlüsselanhänger, sondern wiederaufladbare Feuerzeuge o.ä.

- nö

- keine

- Mailing

- rein faktische Aufklärung sowie eine
ehrliche Beschreibung der Produkte

- Mehr Service beim Kauf von Produkten im Fachhandel und Kaufhäusern

- eine, in der der Mensch mit einbezogen wird tätig zu werden. z.B. sofort testen mit Frage- und Antwortmöglichkeiten oder kreative Mitmachmöglichkeiten.

- mehr produktproben, um produkt vor kauf testen zu können und fehlkäufe zu vermeiden

- kostenloses Lottospielen (Fluxx, tipp24), Werbeaufkleber für Auto (bspw. Freiflug germanwings)

- mehr Kundenorientiertheit allgemein

- nein

- grundsätzlich bin ich für mehr humor beim werben, aber habe nichts konkretes als maßnahme vorzuschlagen

- Bei Einkauf von (z.B) Lebensmittel ab einer bestimmten Summe, Rabatt auf anderweitige Produkte (z.B. Benzin) erhalten... (verbreitete Maßnahme in Australien :))

- stimmende Preisleistungsverhältnisse

- Auch andere Produkte (Chips z.B.)als immer nur Autos sollten öfters mal mit echt geilen Hostessen beworben werden!

- Kundenbindung durch gutes Aftersales.

- Kostenloser Lieferservice nach Hause für "größere Mengen".

- intelligente werbung ohne stereotypen

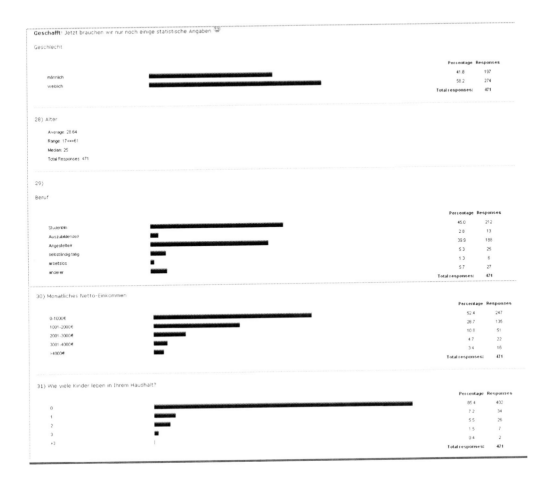

Geschafft! Jetzt brauchen wir nur noch einige statistische Angaben

Geschlecht

	Percentage	Responses
männlich	41.8	197
weiblich	58.2	274
Total responses:		471

28) Alter

Average: 28.64
Range: 17<=>61
Median: 25
Total Responses: 471

29)

Beruf

	Percentage	Responses
Student/in	45.0	212
Auszubildende/r	2.8	13
Angestellte/r	39.9	188
selbständig tätig	5.3	25
arbeitslos	1.3	6
anderer	5.7	27
Total responses:		471

30) Monatliches Netto-Einkommen

	Percentage	Responses
0-1000€	52.4	247
1001-2000€	28.7	135
2001-3000€	10.8	51
3001-4000€	4.7	22
>4000€	3.4	16
Total responses:		471

31) Wie viele Kinder leben in Ihrem Haushalt?

	Percentage	Responses
0	85.4	402
1	7.2	34
2	5.5	26
3	1.5	7
>3	0.4	2
Total responses:		471

II – Filters

Question 1 & 2

1) Female Respondents

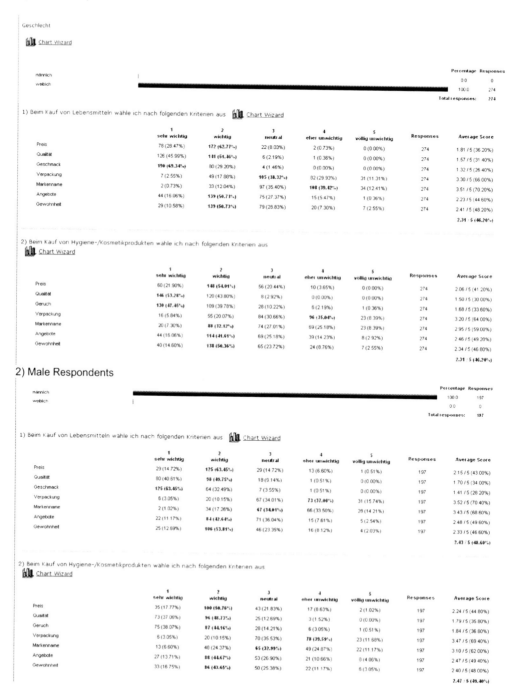

Geschlecht

📊 Chart Wizard

		Percentage	Responses
männlich		0.0	0
weiblich		100.0	274
		Total responses:	274

1) Beim Kauf von Lebensmitteln wähle ich nach folgenden Kriterien aus 📊 Chart Wizard

	1 sehr wichtig	2 wichtig	3 neutral	4 eher unwichtig	5 völlig unwichtig	Responses	Average Score
Preis	78 (28.47%)	172 (62.77%)	22 (8.03%)	2 (0.73%)	0 (0.00%)	274	1.81 / 5 (36.20%)
Qualität	126 (45.99%)	141 (51.46%)	6 (2.19%)	1 (0.36%)	0 (0.00%)	274	1.57 / 5 (31.40%)
Geschmack	190 (69.34%)	80 (29.20%)	4 (1.46%)	0 (0.00%)	0 (0.00%)	274	1.32 / 5 (26.40%)
Verpackung	7 (2.55%)	49 (17.88%)	105 (38.32%)	82 (29.93%)	31 (11.31%)	274	3.30 / 5 (66.00%)
Markenname	2 (0.73%)	33 (12.04%)	97 (35.40%)	108 (39.42%)	34 (12.41%)	274	3.51 / 5 (70.20%)
Angebote	44 (16.06%)	139 (50.73%)	75 (27.37%)	15 (5.47%)	1 (0.36%)	274	2.23 / 5 (44.60%)
Gewohnheit	29 (10.58%)	139 (50.73%)	79 (28.83%)	20 (7.30%)	7 (2.55%)	274	2.41 / 5 (48.20%)
							2.31 : 5 (46.20%)

2) Beim Kauf von Hygiene-/Kosmetikprodukten wähle ich nach folgenden Kriterien aus
📊 Chart Wizard

	1 sehr wichtig	2 wichtig	3 neutral	4 eher unwichtig	5 völlig unwichtig	Responses	Average Score
Preis	60 (21.90%)	148 (54.01%)	56 (20.44%)	10 (3.65%)	0 (0.00%)	274	2.06 / 5 (41.20%)
Qualität	146 (53.28%)	120 (43.80%)	8 (2.92%)	0 (0.00%)	0 (0.00%)	274	1.50 / 5 (30.00%)
Geruch	130 (47.45%)	109 (39.78%)	28 (10.22%)	6 (2.19%)	1 (0.36%)	274	1.68 / 5 (33.60%)
Verpackung	16 (5.84%)	55 (20.07%)	84 (30.66%)	96 (35.04%)	23 (8.39%)	274	3.20 / 5 (64.00%)
Markenname	20 (7.30%)	88 (32.12%)	74 (27.01%)	69 (25.18%)	23 (8.39%)	274	2.95 / 5 (59.00%)
Angebote	44 (16.06%)	114 (41.61%)	69 (25.18%)	39 (14.23%)	8 (2.92%)	274	2.46 / 5 (49.20%)
Gewohnheit	40 (14.60%)	138 (50.36%)	65 (23.72%)	24 (8.76%)	7 (2.55%)	274	2.34 / 5 (46.80%)
							2.31 : 5 (46.20%)

2) Male Respondents

		Percentage	Responses
männlich		100.0	197
weiblich		0.0	0
		Total responses:	197

1) Beim Kauf von Lebensmitteln wähle ich nach folgenden Kriterien aus 📊 Chart Wizard

	1 sehr wichtig	2 wichtig	3 neutral	4 eher unwichtig	5 völlig unwichtig	Responses	Average Score
Preis	29 (14.72%)	125 (63.45%)	29 (14.72%)	13 (6.60%)	1 (0.51%)	197	2.15 / 5 (43.00%)
Qualität	80 (40.61%)	98 (49.75%)	18 (9.14%)	1 (0.51%)	0 (0.00%)	197	1.70 / 5 (34.00%)
Geschmack	125 (63.45%)	64 (32.49%)	7 (3.55%)	1 (0.51%)	0 (0.00%)	197	1.41 / 5 (28.20%)
Verpackung	6 (3.05%)	20 (10.15%)	67 (34.01%)	73 (37.06%)	31 (15.74%)	197	3.52 / 5 (70.40%)
Markenname	2 (1.02%)	34 (17.26%)	67 (34.01%)	66 (33.50%)	28 (14.21%)	197	3.43 / 5 (68.60%)
Angebote	22 (11.17%)	84 (42.64%)	71 (36.04%)	15 (7.61%)	5 (2.54%)	197	2.48 / 5 (49.60%)
Gewohnheit	25 (12.69%)	106 (53.81%)	46 (23.35%)	16 (8.12%)	4 (2.03%)	197	2.33 / 5 (46.60%)
							2.43 / 5 (48.60%)

2) Beim Kauf von Hygiene-/Kosmetikprodukten wähle ich nach folgenden Kriterien aus
📊 Chart Wizard

	1 sehr wichtig	2 wichtig	3 neutral	4 eher unwichtig	5 völlig unwichtig	Responses	Average Score
Preis	35 (17.77%)	100 (50.76%)	43 (21.83%)	17 (8.63%)	2 (1.02%)	197	2.24 / 5 (44.80%)
Qualität	73 (37.06%)	96 (48.73%)	25 (12.69%)	3 (1.52%)	0 (0.00%)	197	1.79 / 5 (35.80%)
Geruch	75 (38.07%)	87 (44.16%)	28 (14.21%)	6 (3.05%)	1 (0.51%)	197	1.84 / 5 (36.80%)
Verpackung	6 (3.05%)	20 (10.15%)	70 (35.53%)	78 (39.59%)	23 (11.68%)	197	3.47 / 5 (69.40%)
Markenname	13 (6.60%)	48 (24.37%)	65 (32.99%)	49 (24.87%)	22 (11.17%)	197	3.10 / 5 (62.00%)
Angebote	27 (13.71%)	88 (44.67%)	53 (26.90%)	21 (10.66%)	8 (4.06%)	197	2.47 / 5 (49.40%)
Gewohnheit	33 (16.75%)	86 (43.65%)	50 (25.38%)	22 (11.17%)	6 (3.05%)	197	2.40 / 5 (48.00%)
							2.47 : 5 (49.40%)

Question 3

1) Female Respondents

3) Wie wichtig ist es für Sie die folgenden Produkte vor dem Kauf zu testen? 📊 Chart Wizard

	1 sehr wichtig	2 wichtig	3 neutral	4 eher unwichtig	5 völlig unwichtig	Responses	Average Score
Snacks/Süßigkeiten	7 (2.55%)	48 (17.52%)	89 (32.48%)	106 (38.69%)	24 (8.76%)	274	3.34 / 5 (66.80%)
Joghurt/Pudding	6 (2.19%)	45 (16.42%)	95 (34.67%)	106 (38.69%)	22 (8.03%)	274	3.34 / 5 (66.80%)
Suppen/Soßen	8 (2.92%)	38 (13.87%)	94 (34.31%)	108 (39.42%)	26 (9.49%)	274	3.39 / 5 (67.80%)
Aufschnitt	11 (4.01%)	58 (21.17%)	110 (40.15%)	76 (27.74%)	19 (6.93%)	274	3.12 / 5 (62.40%)
Backwaren	13 (4.74%)	58 (21.17%)	95 (34.67%)	91 (33.21%)	17 (6.20%)	274	3.15 / 5 (63.00%)
Getränke	12 (4.38%)	68 (24.82%)	98 (35.77%)	80 (29.20%)	16 (5.84%)	274	3.07 / 5 (61.40%)
Hygiene-/Kosmetikprodukte	53 (19.34%)	126 (45.99%)	52 (18.98%)	34 (12.41%)	9 (3.28%)	274	2.34 / 5 (46.80%)
Software/Internetanbieter	60 (21.90%)	98 (35.77%)	71 (25.91%)	29 (10.58%)	16 (5.84%)	274	2.43 / 5 (48.60%)
Zeitungen/Zeitschriften	41 (14.96%)	109 (39.78%)	69 (25.18%)	35 (12.77%)	20 (7.30%)	274	2.58 / 5 (51.60%)
							2.97 / 5 (59.40%)

2) Male Respondents

3) Wie wichtig ist es für Sie die folgenden Produkte vor dem Kauf zu testen? 📊 Chart Wizard

	1 sehr wichtig	2 wichtig	3 neutral	4 eher unwichtig	5 völlig unwichtig	Responses	Average Score
Snacks/Süßigkeiten	4 (2.03%)	49 (24.87%)	58 (29.44%)	59 (29.95%)	27 (13.71%)	197	3.28 / 5 (65.60%)
Joghurt/Pudding	6 (3.05%)	42 (21.32%)	60 (30.46%)	68 (34.52%)	21 (10.66%)	197	3.28 / 5 (65.60%)
Suppen/Soßen	4 (2.03%)	34 (17.26%)	55 (27.92%)	79 (40.10%)	25 (12.69%)	197	3.44 / 5 (68.80%)
Aufschnitt	9 (4.57%)	55 (27.92%)	56 (28.43%)	57 (28.93%)	20 (10.15%)	197	3.12 / 5 (62.40%)
Backwaren	6 (3.05%)	37 (18.78%)	67 (34.01%)	66 (33.50%)	21 (10.66%)	197	3.30 / 5 (66.00%)
Getränke	12 (6.09%)	65 (32.99%)	47 (23.86%)	53 (26.90%)	20 (10.15%)	197	3.02 / 5 (60.40%)
Hygiene-/Kosmetikprodukte	19 (9.64%)	58 (29.44%)	59 (29.95%)	42 (21.32%)	19 (9.64%)	197	2.92 / 5 (58.40%)
Software/Internetanbieter	50 (25.38%)	72 (36.55%)	43 (21.83%)	23 (11.68%)	9 (4.57%)	197	2.34 / 5 (46.80%)
Zeitungen/Zeitschriften	34 (17.26%)	93 (47.21%)	33 (16.75%)	23 (11.68%)	14 (7.11%)	197	2.44 / 5 (48.80%)
							3.02 / 5 (60.40%)

Question 4

1) Female Respondents

4) Ich nehme Produktproben mit weil... 📊 Chart Wizard

	1 immer	2 oft	3 manchmal	4 selten	5 nie	Responses	Average Score
ich interessiert an Qualität/Geschmack bin	59 (21.53%)	125 (45.62%)	66 (24.09%)	19 (6.93%)	5 (1.82%)	274	2.22 / 5 (44.40%)
sie gratis sind	93 (33.94%)	82 (29.93%)	61 (22.26%)	31 (11.31%)	7 (2.55%)	274	2.19 / 5 (43.80%)
es sich um neue Produkte handelt	52 (18.98%)	110 (40.15%)	76 (27.74%)	27 (9.85%)	9 (3.28%)	274	2.38 / 5 (47.60%)
							2.26 / 5 (45.20%)

2) Male Respondents

4) Ich nehme Produktproben mit weil... 📊 Chart Wizard

	1 immer	2 oft	3 manchmal	4 selten	5 nie	Responses	Average Score
ich interessiert an Qualität/Geschmack bin	19 (9.64%)	75 (38.07%)	58 (29.44%)	29 (14.72%)	16 (8.12%)	197	2.74 / 5 (54.80%)
sie gratis sind	37 (18.78%)	70 (35.53%)	44 (22.34%)	26 (13.20%)	20 (10.15%)	197	2.60 / 5 (52.00%)
es sich um neue Produkte handelt	23 (11.68%)	71 (36.04%)	55 (27.92%)	28 (14.21%)	20 (10.15%)	197	2.75 / 5 (55.00%)
							2.70 / 5 (54.00%)

Question 9 & 10

1) Coca-Cola

2) Pepsi

Question 11

1) Female respondents

2) Male respondents

Question 17

1) Female respondents

2) Male respondents

3) Filter: very much

Question 20

1) Premium

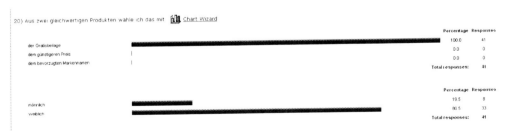

5) Wenn mich ein Probchen überzeugt hat, kaufe ich das Produkt beim nächsten Bedarf   Chart Wizard

	Percentage	Responses
immer	4.9	2
oft	43.9	18
manchmal	43.9	18
selten	7.3	3
nie	0.0	0
	Total responses:	41

15)

Ich bin daran interessiert Coupons auszuschneiden, zu sammeln und einzulösen.

Chart Wizard

	Percentage	Responses
sehr	9.8	4
ein wenig	58.5	24
gar nicht	31.7	13
	Total responses:	41

19) Ich kaufe eine Zeitung/Zeitschrift wegen des Extras/der Beilage   Chart Wizard

	Percentage	Responses
immer	2.4	1
oft	17.1	7
manchmal	46.3	19
selten	24.4	10
nie	9.8	4
	Total responses:	41

2) Preferred brand

20) Aus zwei gleichwertigen Produkten wähle ich das mit   Chart Wizard

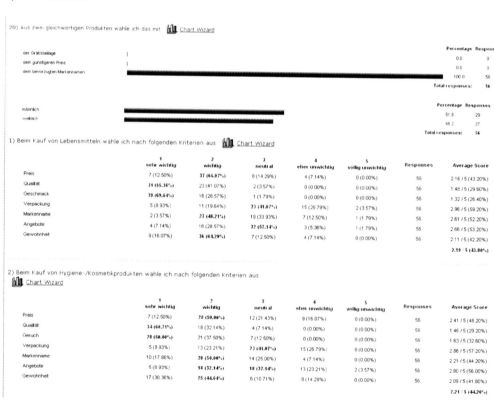

	Percentage	Responses
der Gratisbeilage	0.0	0
dem günstigeren Preis	0.0	0
dem bevorzugten Markennamen	100.0	56
	Total responses:	56

	Percentage	Responses
männlich	51.8	29
weiblich	48.2	27
	Total responses:	56

1) Beim Kauf von Lebensmitteln wähle ich nach folgenden Kriterien aus   Chart Wizard

	1 sehr wichtig	2 wichtig	3 neutral	4 eher unwichtig	5 völlig unwichtig	Responses	Average Score
Preis	7 (12.50%)	37 (66.07%)	8 (14.29%)	4 (7.14%)	0 (0.00%)	56	2.16 / 5 (43.20%)
Qualität	31 (55.36%)	23 (41.07%)	2 (3.57%)	0 (0.00%)	0 (0.00%)	56	1.48 / 5 (29.60%)
Geschmack	39 (69.64%)	16 (28.57%)	1 (1.79%)	0 (0.00%)	0 (0.00%)	56	1.32 / 5 (26.40%)
Verpackung	5 (8.93%)	11 (19.64%)	23 (41.07%)	15 (26.79%)	2 (3.57%)	56	2.96 / 5 (59.20%)
Markenname	2 (3.57%)	27 (48.21%)	19 (33.93%)	7 (12.50%)	1 (1.79%)	56	2.61 / 5 (52.20%)
Angebote	4 (7.14%)	16 (28.57%)	32 (57.14%)	3 (5.36%)	1 (1.79%)	56	2.66 / 5 (53.20%)
Gewohnheit	9 (16.07%)	36 (64.29%)	7 (12.50%)	4 (7.14%)	0 (0.00%)	56	2.11 / 5 (42.20%)
							2.19 / 5 (43.80%)

2) Beim Kauf von Hygiene-/Kosmetikprodukten wähle ich nach folgenden Kriterien aus
   Chart Wizard

	1 sehr wichtig	2 wichtig	3 neutral	4 eher unwichtig	5 völlig unwichtig	Responses	Average Score
Preis	7 (12.50%)	28 (50.00%)	12 (21.43%)	9 (16.07%)	0 (0.00%)	56	2.41 / 5 (48.20%)
Qualität	34 (60.71%)	18 (32.14%)	4 (7.14%)	0 (0.00%)	0 (0.00%)	56	1.46 / 5 (29.20%)
Geruch	28 (50.00%)	21 (37.50%)	7 (12.50%)	0 (0.00%)	0 (0.00%)	56	1.63 / 5 (32.60%)
Verpackung	5 (8.93%)	13 (23.21%)	23 (41.07%)	15 (26.79%)	0 (0.00%)	56	2.86 / 5 (57.20%)
Markenname	10 (17.86%)	28 (50.00%)	14 (25.00%)	4 (7.14%)	0 (0.00%)	56	2.21 / 5 (44.20%)
Angebote	5 (8.93%)	18 (32.14%)	18 (32.14%)	13 (23.21%)	2 (3.57%)	56	2.80 / 5 (56.00%)
Gewohnheit	17 (30.36%)	25 (44.64%)	6 (10.71%)	8 (14.29%)	0 (0.00%)	56	2.09 / 5 (41.80%)
							2.21 / 5 (44.20%)

30) Monatliches Netto-Einkommen  Chart Wizard

	Percentage	Responses
0-1000€	37.5	21
1001-2000€	39.3	22
2001-3000€	10.7	6
3001-4000€	5.4	3
>4000€	7.1	4
	Total responses:	56

3) Female respondents

20) Aus zwei gleichwertigen Produkten wahle ich das mit  Chart Wizard

	Percentage	Responses
der Gratisbeilage	12.0	33
dem günstigeren Preis	78.1	214
dem bevorzugten Markennamen	9.9	27
	Total responses:	274

4) Male respondents

20) Aus zwei gleichwertigen Produkten wahle ich das mit 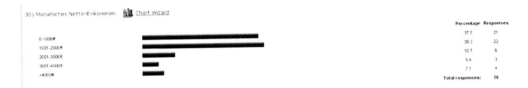 Chart Wizard

	Percentage	Responses
der Gratisbeilage	4.1	8
dem günstigeren Preis	81.2	160
dem bevorzugten Markennamen	14.7	29
	Total responses:	197

Printed in the United Kingdom by
Lightning Source UK Ltd., Milton Keynes
139040UK00001B/10/A